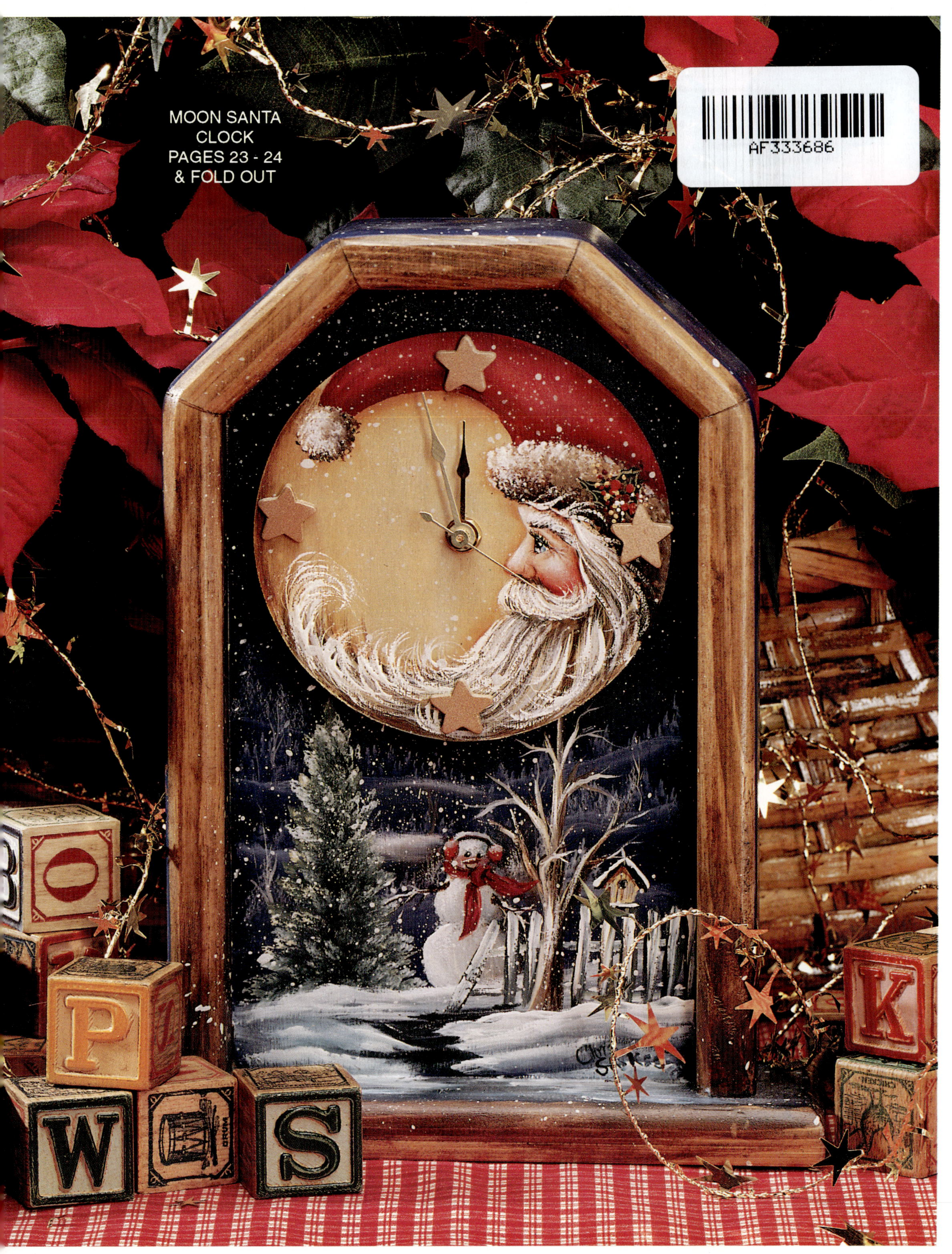

MOON SANTA
CLOCK
PAGES 23 - 24
& FOLD OUT

AF333686

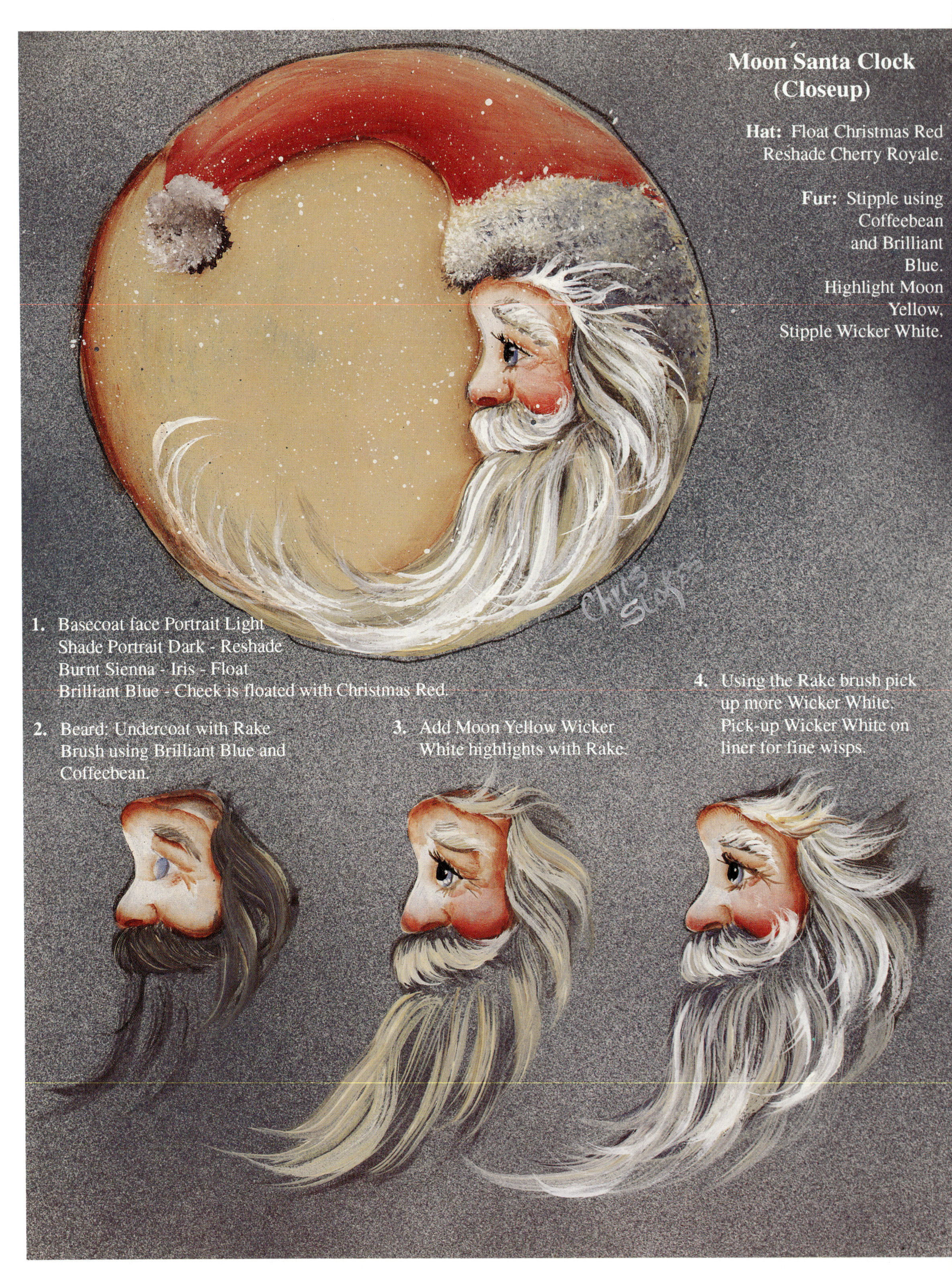

Moon Santa Clock
(Closeup)

Hat: Float Christmas Red
Reshade Cherry Royale.

Fur: Stipple using
Coffeebean
and Brilliant
Blue.
Highlight Moon
Yellow,
Stipple Wicker White.

1. Basecoat face Portrait Light
Shade Portrait Dark - Reshade
Burnt Sienna - Iris - Float
Brilliant Blue - Cheek is floated with Christmas Red.

2. Beard: Undercoat with Rake
Brush using Brilliant Blue and
Coffeebean.

3. Add Moon Yellow Wicker
White highlights with Rake.

4. Using the Rake brush pick
up more Wicker White.
Pick-up Wicker White on
liner for fine wisps.

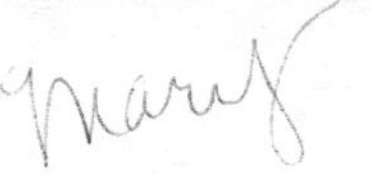

Copyright © 1995 Susan Scheewe Publications
13435 N.E. Whitaker Way, Portland, OR 97230
Phone (503) 254-9100 Fax (503) 252-9508

1

Meet the Author

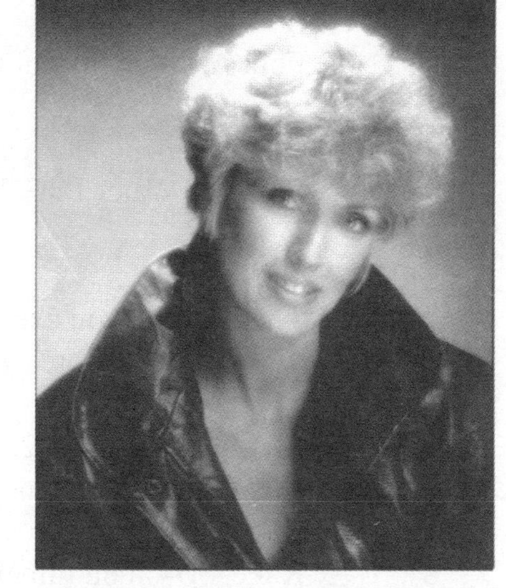

Chris Stokes has been painting for more than a decade. She says, "I am a self-taught artist without any fancy credentials, but I do love to paint." And as you can see, her work speaks for itself.

Ten years ago, Chris opened a quaint little craft/gift shop nestled in downtown Dallas, Ga. Many of the items to paint shown in this book are available from Chris's shop, The Craft Cottage. With much hard work and self education, this shop is now a thriving business. Chris and her staff teach craft courses of all types and have fun helping their customers CREATE.

Chris says that "Living in a log home in Dallas, Georgia with my husband, Ron, son, James (age 23), and daughter, Jennifer, (age 21) makes life lots of fun. Two cats and four dogs complete my family."

For information on classes and supplies, contact:
The Craft Cottage
222 Main Street
Dallas, Georgia 30132
(770) 445-8228

Dedication

I dedicate this book (my ninth) to all those cherished customers, students, fellow painters and friends. Thanks so much for you support and encouragement. Without you my books would not be possible.

Also a special thanks goes to Ricky, my sweet little wood man, Plaid Enterprises, Inc. for publishing books for me, Susan Scheewe for publishing this book and last but not least the lord for blessing me so generously.

Special Note: *Relax and enjoy this, my third Christmas Book. May it bring many hours of pleasure. Have Yourself a Merry Little Christmas!!!*

Look for Chris's other Plaid books:
Painted Enchantments (Plaid #8704)
Craft Cottage Christmas (Plaid #8705)
From an Enchanted Garden (Plaid #8811)
The Cottage Collection (Plaid #8909)
The Pleasures of Country Life (Plaid #8948)
Christmas Cottage Painting Joys (Plaid #8949)
Simply Gourd-geous (Plaid #8907)
My Cottage Garden (Plaid #9170)

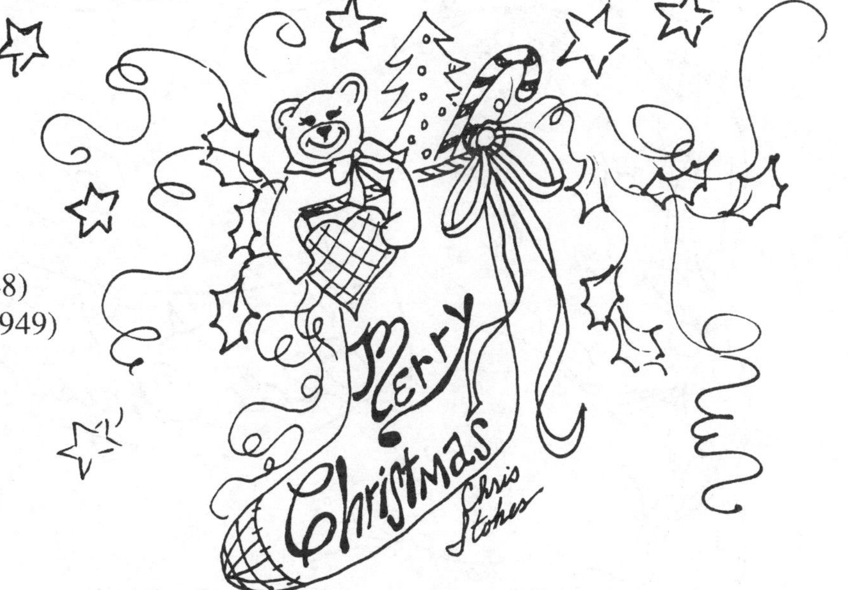

Supplies You Will Need

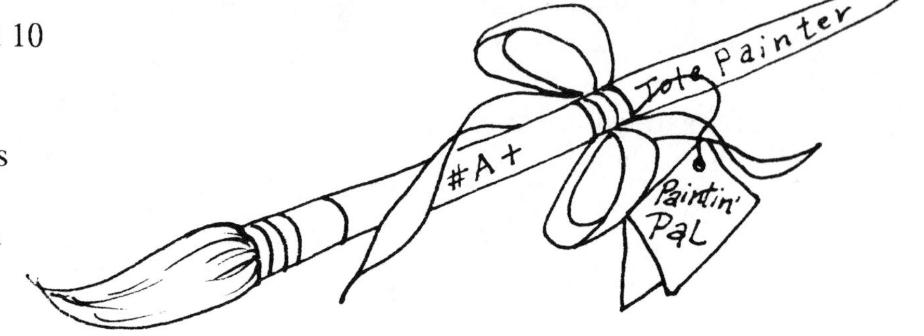

PAINTS

    Folk Art Acrylic Colors and Pure Pigment Colors

SEALER

    Folk Art Water Base Varnish

BRUSHES

    The brushes you use are important tools in achieving a successfully painted design - so shop for the best you can afford. I use Betty Byrd or Folk Art brushes.

    Flat Shaders: Nos. 2, 4, 6, 8 and 10
    Liner and Script Liner
    Round No. 3
    Rake - 1/4 Inch Filbert and Flats
    Glaze - 1/2 and 3/4 Inch
    Stencil Brush - 1/2 and 3/4 Inch
    Old Scruffy Brush

WOOD ITEMS TO PAINT

    Many wood items are available through our shop and many other craft shops. Patterns are provided for many items if you prefer to cut your own.

    The Craft Cottage
    222 Main Street
    Dallas, Ga. 30132
    (404) 445-8228

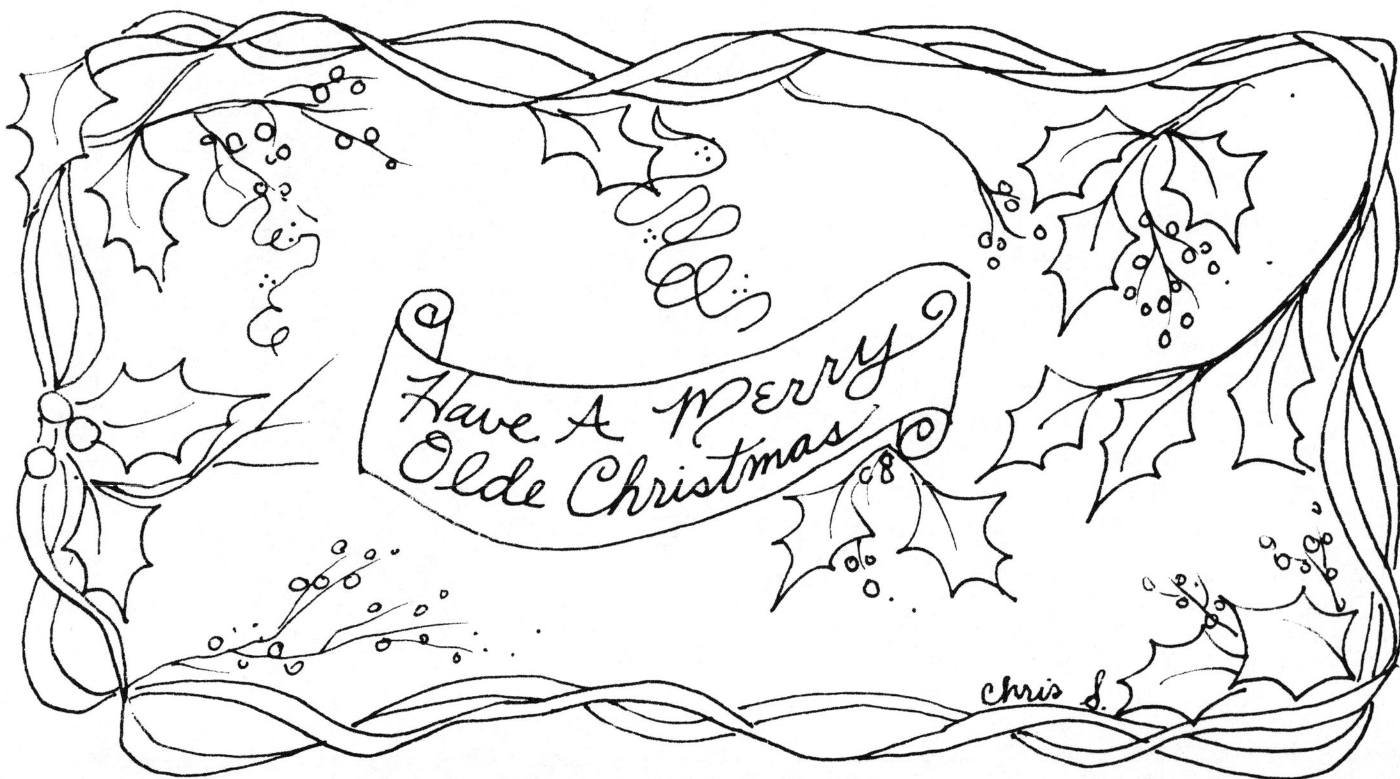

Painting Tips

BASIC WOOD PAINTING PROCEDURE

When painting on wood, follow the same step-by-step procedure with each piece. The following are simple steps (given in order) that you need to follow to create a truly beautiful painted item.

1. **SANDING AND TACKING:** Sand the wood with fine sandpaper in the direction of the grain, then wipe it with a tack cloth to remove dust and fibers. (NOTE: I rarely seal my wood because the basecoat takes better on raw wood.)

2. **BASECOATING:** Load a sponge brush or a large flat brush with the paint color specified for the basecoat in the instructions. With long even strokes , paint your wood, stroking in the direction of the grain. Sometimes more than one coat will be needed (if so, "sand" with a paper sack before repainting - see next step). Some projects are stained with antiquing instead of being basecoated.

3. **"SANDING" WITH A PAPER SACK:** This is done after the basecoat has dried. Cut a heavy brown paper grocery sack into medium size (approximately 6" x 6") pieces. Use these to "sand" over the dry basecoat. This polishes the fibers back down into the wood and makes the design painting go much easier. If a second basecoat is applied, let it dry, then repeat the paper sack sanding.

4. **TRACING AND TRANSFERRING THE PATTERN:** First trace the pattern from the book onto tracing paper. To do this, place the tracing paper over the pattern and carefully trace the major parts only; they are all that will need to be transferred. The detailed pattern in the book can be used for visual guidance as you paint.
    Place the traced pattern in position on the item to be painted and tape it in place, leaving one side untaped. Slide transfer paper with the shiny side down under the tracing paper. Then trace over the major lines with a stylus to transfer the pattern.

5. **DESIGN PAINTING:** Paint the design following the project instructions, using the painting techniques given later in this section.

6. **SPATTERING:** some projects are spattered or speckled after the design painting is complete and dry. Load an old toothbrush with water. Shake out excess water. Place the bristles in a puddle of paint, blot on a paper towel, aim carefully toward the project, and pull your fingernail across the bristles to release specks of paint. Test on newspaper or scrap paper before doing this on your project. Let dry.

7. **FINISHING:** Varnish the wood projects with one or two coats of Folk Art ® Water Base Varnish

8. **CLEANING BRUSHES:** Always keep your brushes clean. Flats should have a fine chisel edge; rounds and liners should come to a very fine point. To achieve this, always clean your brushes with Brush Plus ® brush cleaner, removing all paint. If you have very stubborn paint, dip the brush in rubbing alcohol. This will soften even the oldest dried paint. (It works well to remove paint from fingernails, too.) Then put Brush Plus® back in the brush and reshape. Leave it in the brush till next use, then rinse it out of the brush before using.

Painting Terms and Techniques

DOUBLE LOAD

Load half of the brush with one color of paint and the other half with another color. Stroke the brush on the palette until the colors gently blend where they meet in the brush and yet remain unblended on each side of the brush.

FLOATED OR SIDELOADED COLOR

This method is used for shading and highlighting. Dip a flat brush into water and blot once on a paper towel. Load only the left corner tip of the brush with paint. Stroke the brush back and forth on the palette so that the paint blends gradually into the water. Paint should gradually flow across the brush but not all the way across - no paint should be on the right corner of the brush.

DRYBRUSH

Dip the brush into a tiny bit of paint. Brush on a paper towel to remove excess paint. Brush lightly on your project.

"INKY"

Mix lots of water with paint on your palette until it has the consistency of ink. Paint used on a liner brush should have this consistency. (If you can write your name without reloading you have done it right.)

SCRUFFY BRUSH

This is an old brush that has "flared out" - the bristles no longer return to the original shape of the brush but continue to stick out. It is not good for most decorative painting, but good for stippling. (Using it will also keep you from ruining a good brush with the stippling process.)

STIPPLING

Load either an old scruffy brush or a small stencil brush with paint by pouncing it up and down in paint on the palette. (I usually load two or three colors together at a time.) The paint needs to be kept pretty dry. Pounce the brush once or twice on a paper towel to be sure there is not too much paint in it, then pounce the brush up and down on your project. This technique is used to paint the suggestion of bushes and general greenery areas.

MAKING DOTS

These can be made with either a stylus or the handle end of a small brush. Dip the stylus or brush handle into a puddle of paint, then touch it on your project where you want the dot. If you want dots to be all the same size, reload the stylus with paint for each dot.

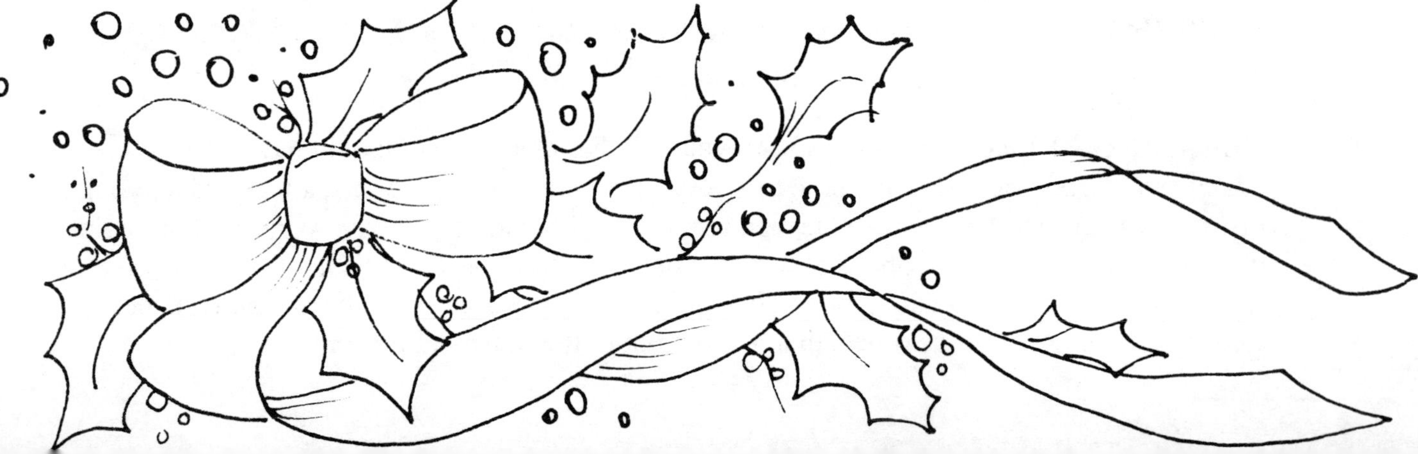

Holly the Christmas Angel

Holly's candle provides a warm greeting to all those holiday visitors.

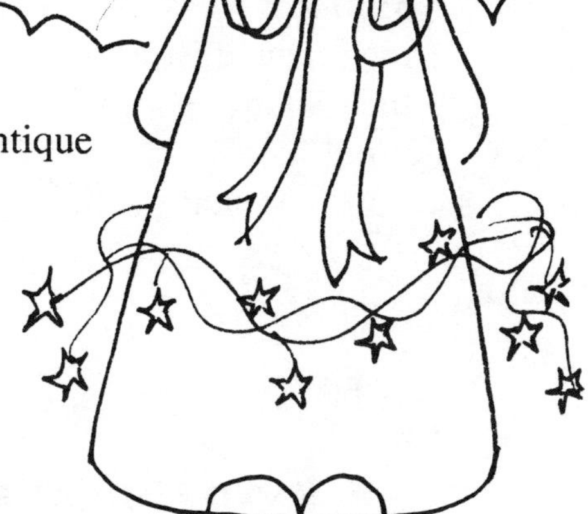

PALETTE

Metallic Gold
Skintone
Clay Bisque
Brownie
Warm White
Folk Art Crackle Medium

Teddy Bear Brown
Dapple Gray
Spanish Tile
Hunter Green

BRUSHES

3/4 Inch Glaze
Script Liner
3/4 Inch Stencil Brush
2 Inch Sponge Brush
No. 6 Flat Brush

MISCELLANEOUS

Down Home Brown Antique
Spanish Moss for hair
Holly
Candle
Stylus
Wooden Candle Cup

INSTRUCTIONS

1. **SAND AND TACK WOOD**
Stain all pieces using sponge brush and "inky" Down Home Brown. Let dry. Repaint front surface only with Clay Bisque. Wings are crackled - using Crackle Medium - follow manufacturer directions. Let dry. Repaint surface with Warm White. When dry and crackled, streak with Metallic Gold.

2. **FACE AND HANDS**
Basecoat Skintone - shade Teddy Bear Brown. Using stencil brush (very dry) and Spanish Tile blush cheeks. Eyelashes are "inky" Dapple Gray. Inside mouth is floated in Brownie. Bottom lip is floated in Spanish Tile.

3. **DRESS AND SLEEVES**
Shade with Dapple Gray, highlight with Warm White. Comma strokes on sleeve and collar are painted in using liner brush and Brownie. Metallic gold stylus dots are also added.

4. **HOLLY**
Freehand or stencil holly on dress using Hunter Green. Berries are double loaded No. 6 flat Spanish Tile/Brownie with Warm White highlights. Line work is painted with script liner and "inky" Hunter Green and touch of Brownie. Metallic Gold comma strokes. Spatter with "inky" Metallic Gold.

5. **BASE AND CANDLE HOLDER**
Top is painted Brownie, trim is Hunter Green. Candle cup is Metallic Gold.

6. **FINISH**
Varnish with Water Base Varnish and decorate with holly and ribbons, etc.

Gingerbread Cookie / Cake Holder

A cute way to serve all those yummy goodies.

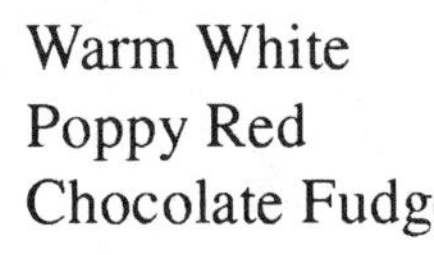

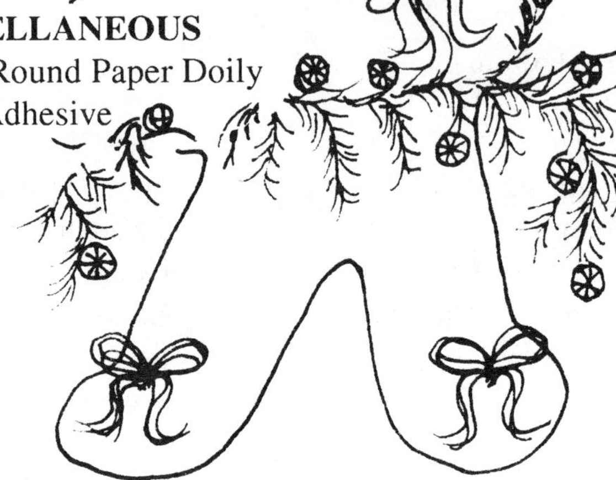

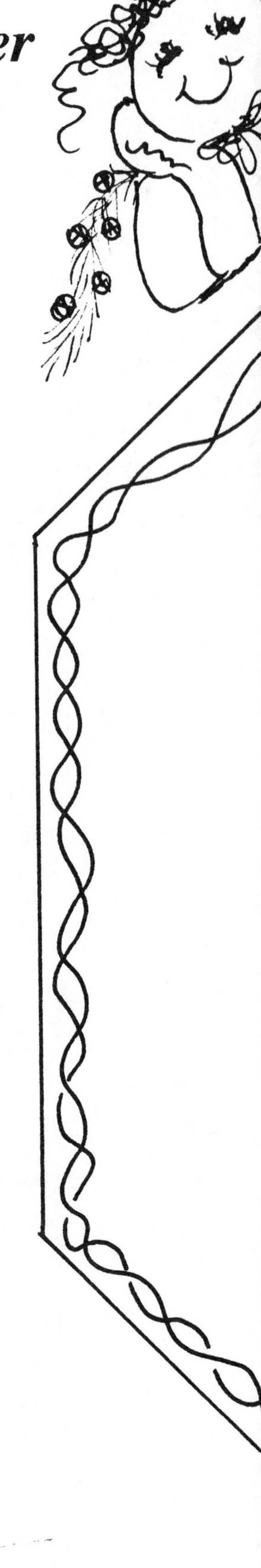

PALETTE

English Mustard
Cherry Royale
Molasses
Shamrock

Warm White
Poppy Red
Chocolate Fudge

BRUSHES

No. 10 Flat
1 Inch Stencil Brush
1 Inch Sponge Brush
Script Liner
1/4 Inch Stencil Brush

MISCELLANEOUS

8 Inch Round Paper Doily
Spray Adhesive

INSTRUCTIONS

1. **SAND AND TACK WOOD**

   "Stain" all pieces with a wash of English Mustard. Let dry. Sand with paper bag.

2. **PLATE HOLDER**

   Paint top surface with 1 inch sponge brush and Warm White. Let dry. Spray adhesive on paper doily. Press down in center of wood. Using 1 inch sten cil brush and Shamrock pounce total surface. Outside edge is trimmed with Cherry Royale. Lift off paper doily.

3. **GINGERBREAD "COOKIES"**

   Shade with Molasses, re-shade with Chocolate Fudge. "Icing" around edges is painted with liner and Warm White. Eyes are painted with Chocolate Fudge and handle end of brush. Warm White highlights. Shade around outside edge of eyes with Molasses. Scarf is painted in with a liner brush and Shamrock, then "wrap" with Cherry Royal; then with Warm White. Nose is Cherry Royal dot. "Plug" (covering the screw) is painted to look like a round peppermint using Warm White and Cherry Royale stripes. Shade outside edge with Chocolate Fudge.

4. **FINISH**

   Varnish with Water Base Varnish (several coats on plate). Wipe clean after use. Do not immerse in water.

Gingerbread Cookie / Cake Holder

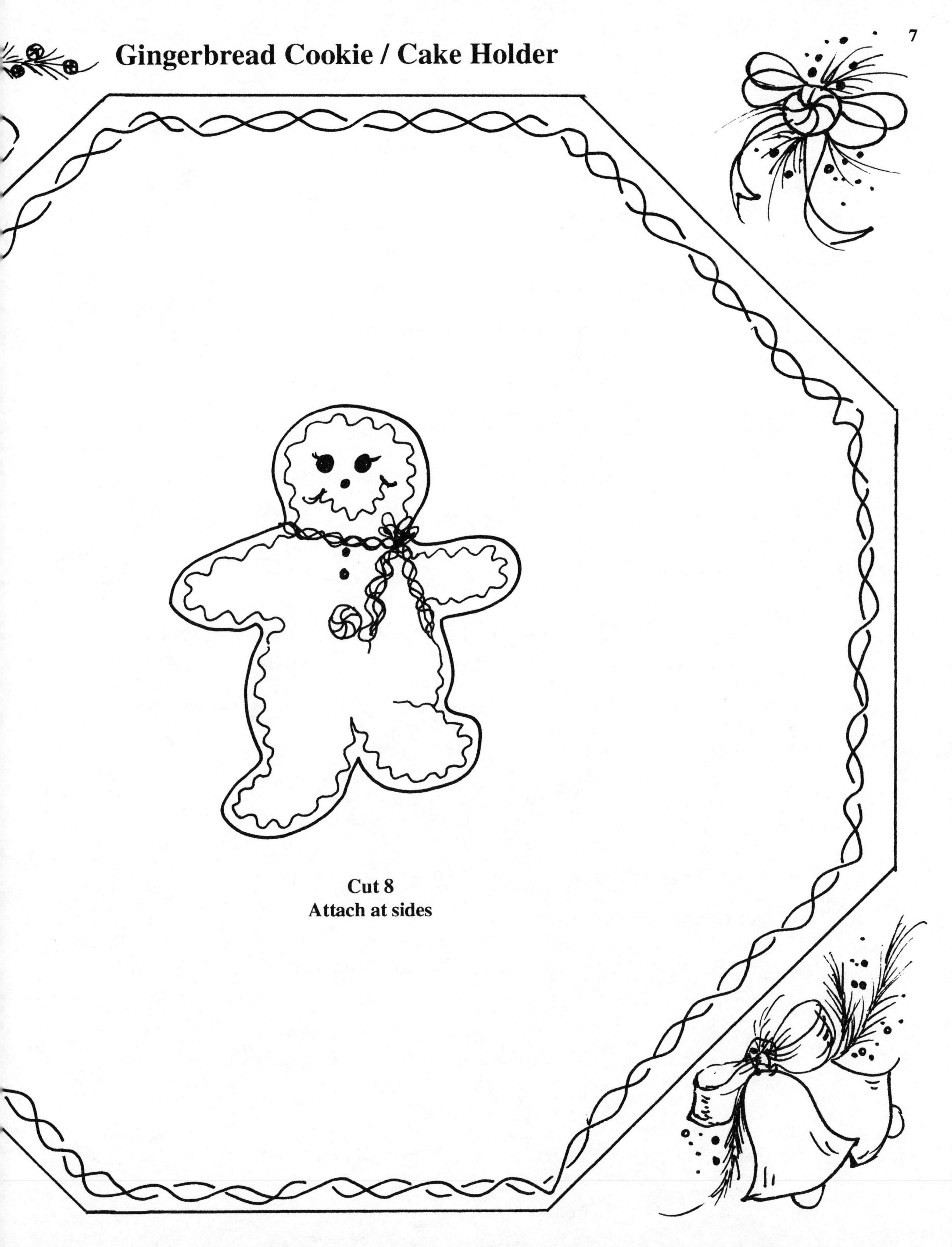

Cut 8
Attach at sides

"Snow Family"

So, cute, gathered together on your mantle!

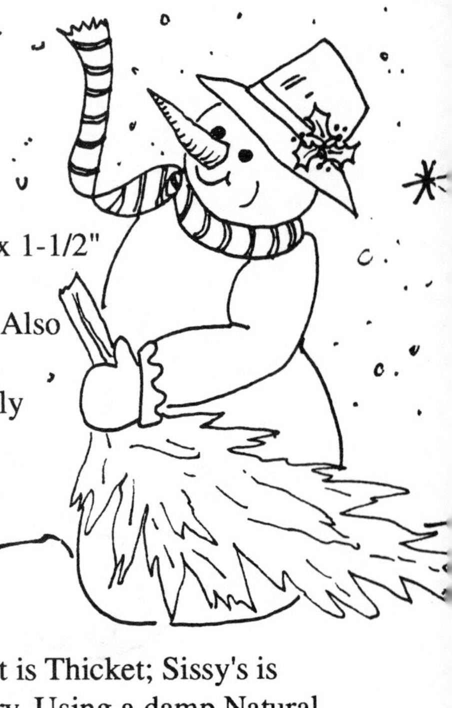

PALETTE

Barnwood	Licorice
Thicket	Apple Spice
Frosted Berry	Tangerine
Warm White	

BRUSHES - Folk Art

1/2 Inch Glaze
Script Liner
Stylus
2 Inch Sponge Brush
Small Stencil Brush
No. 3 Round

MISCELLANEOUS SUPPLIES

Folk Are Water Base Varnish
Four Pieces Plaid Wool Fabric Cut 18" Long x 1-1/2"
Wide For Scarves
Plastic White Branches For Arms (Twigs Are Also
Very Cute)
Miscellaneous Items To Decorate Snow Family
Natural Sponge
Curly White Hair For The Girls
Snow Tex

INSTRUCTIONS

1. **SAND AND TACK WOOD**
   Using a sponge brush, basecoat all bodies in Barnwood. Mama's hat is Thicket; Sissy's is Apple Spice; Papa's is Licorice and Bubba's is Frosted Berry. Let dry. Using a damp Natural Sponge pounce all bodies with Warm White. Shade with Barnwood. Using small stencil brush and very little Apple Spice paint - "blush" all cheeks with circular motion.

2. **"COAL" EYES AND MOUTH**
   All eyes and mouths are "wiggled" in with the handle end of your brush with Licorice. The girl's have eyelashes. Paint Warm White sparkle in the eyes.

3. **CARROT NOSE**
   Double load Tangerine/Apple Spice. Let dry - shade with Apple Spice.

4. **HEART BUTTONS ON GIRLS**
   Painted with handle end of brush using Thicket, Apple Spice, Frosted Berry. Liner brush and Warm White "stitches" the buttons in place. Plain button on boys.

5. **FINISH**
   Varnish with Waterbase Varnish. Hot glue hair on girls and hot glue hats in place. Attach plastic white branch for arms. Decorate with lots of goodies, spatter with Snow Tex and apply some thickly here and there. Be prepared to paint tons of these sweet little snow people.

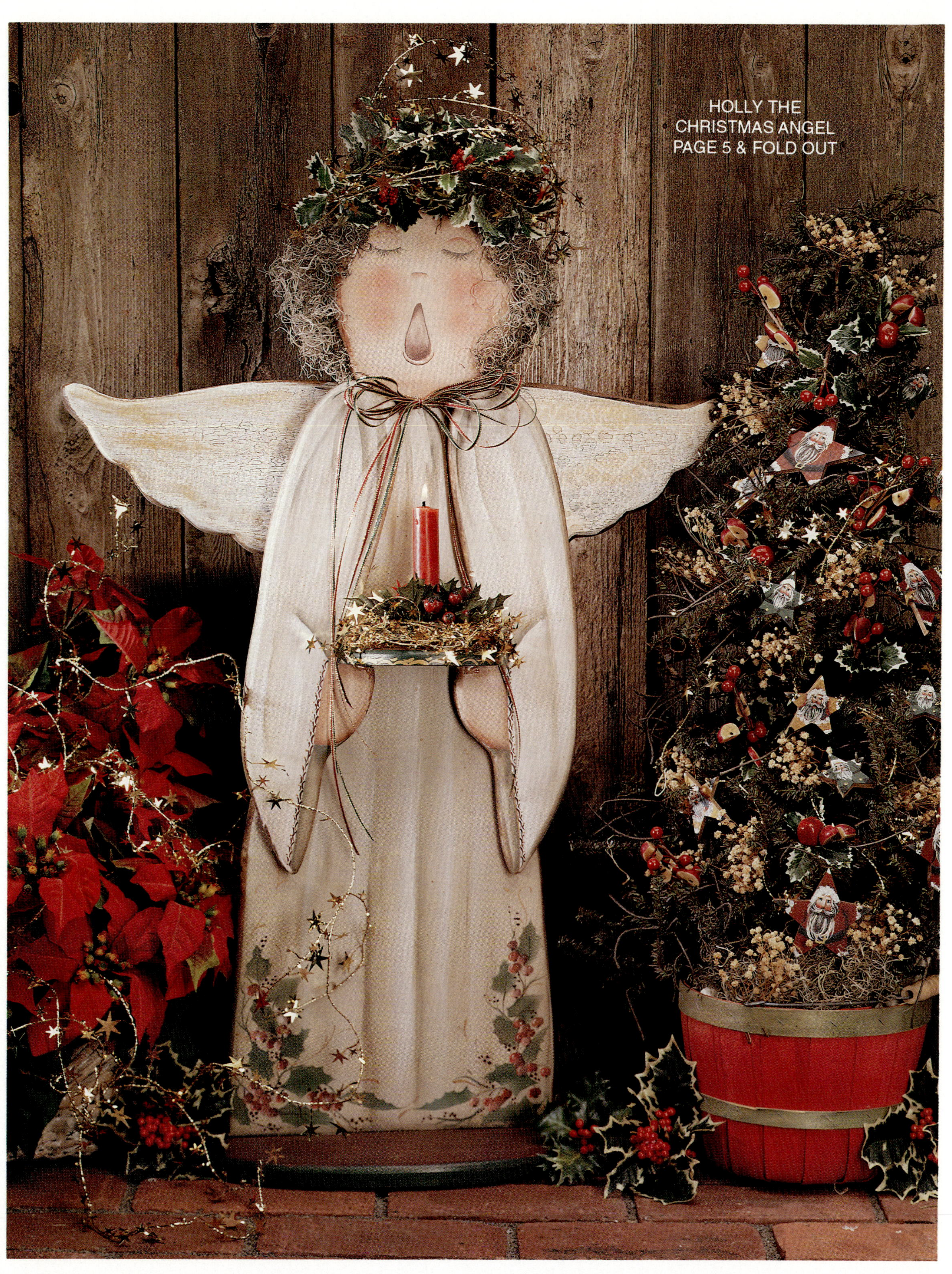
HOLLY THE
CHRISTMAS ANGEL
PAGE 5 & FOLD OUT

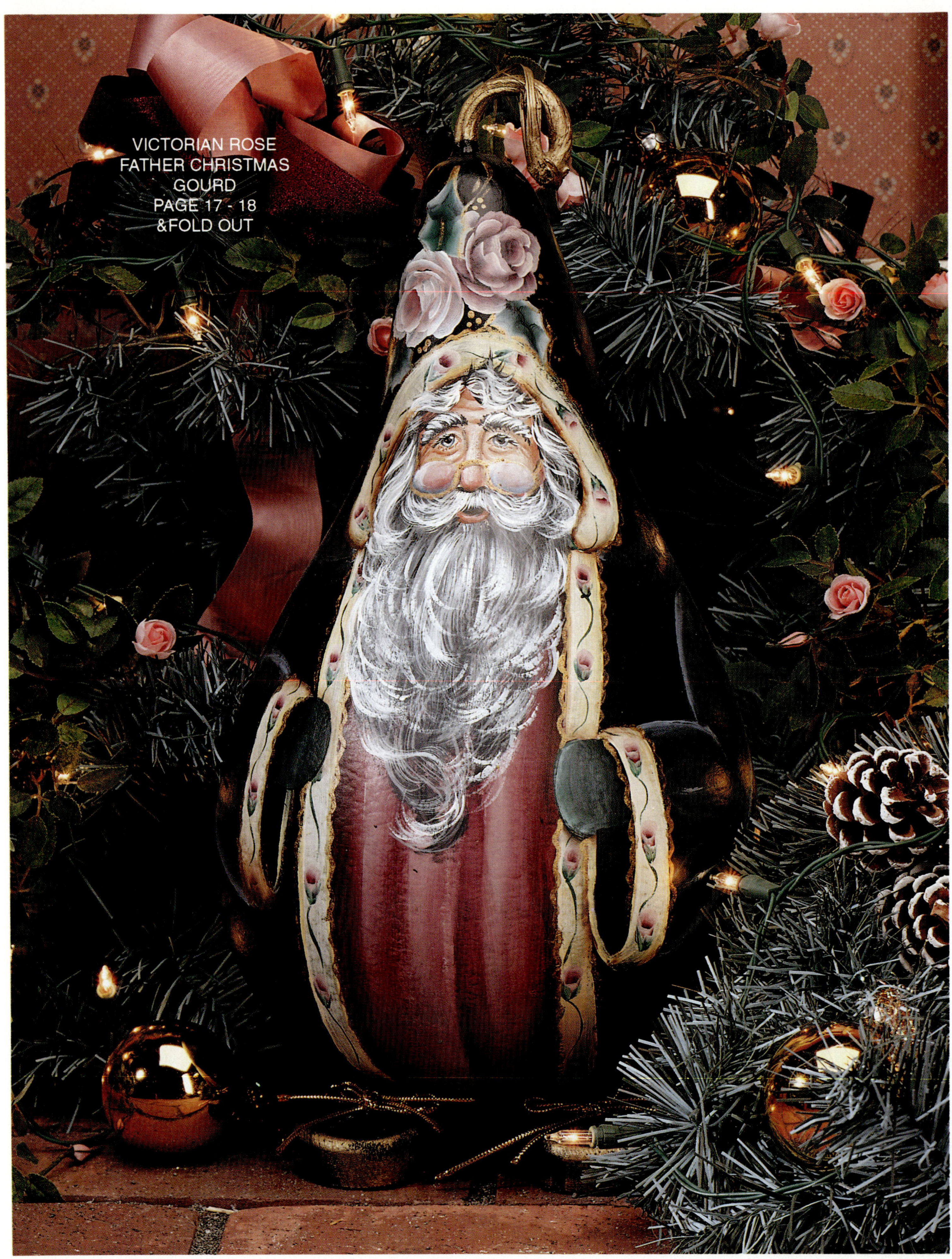

VICTORIAN ROSE
FATHER CHRISTMAS
GOURD
PAGE 17 - 18
&FOLD OUT

Victoria Rose Santa

Double Load #8 Flat
Brush with Taffy and
Burnt Carmen

"Wiggle" in
back petals

Reload...
Wiggle in
middle petals

Reload...pull in
side petals

Reload... pull in petals
to form bowl

Reload...
Pull in filler petals to complete rose.

Double load #8
flat brush with
Emerald Isle & Taffy

Holly Leaf

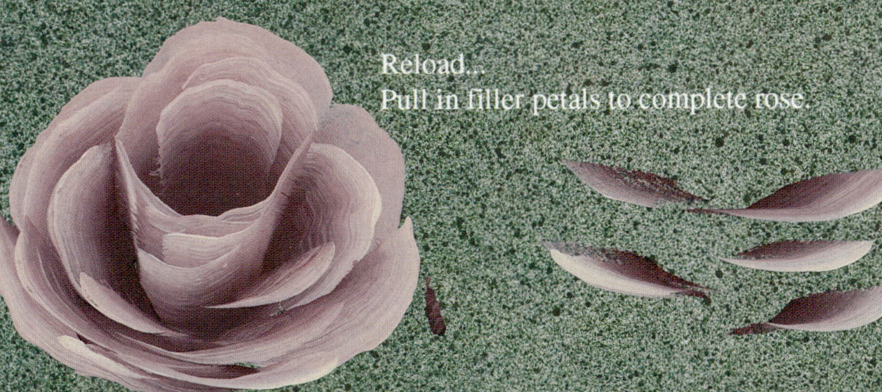

Pull chisel edge of brush
down middle for vein.
Outline in Metallic Gold
with Liner

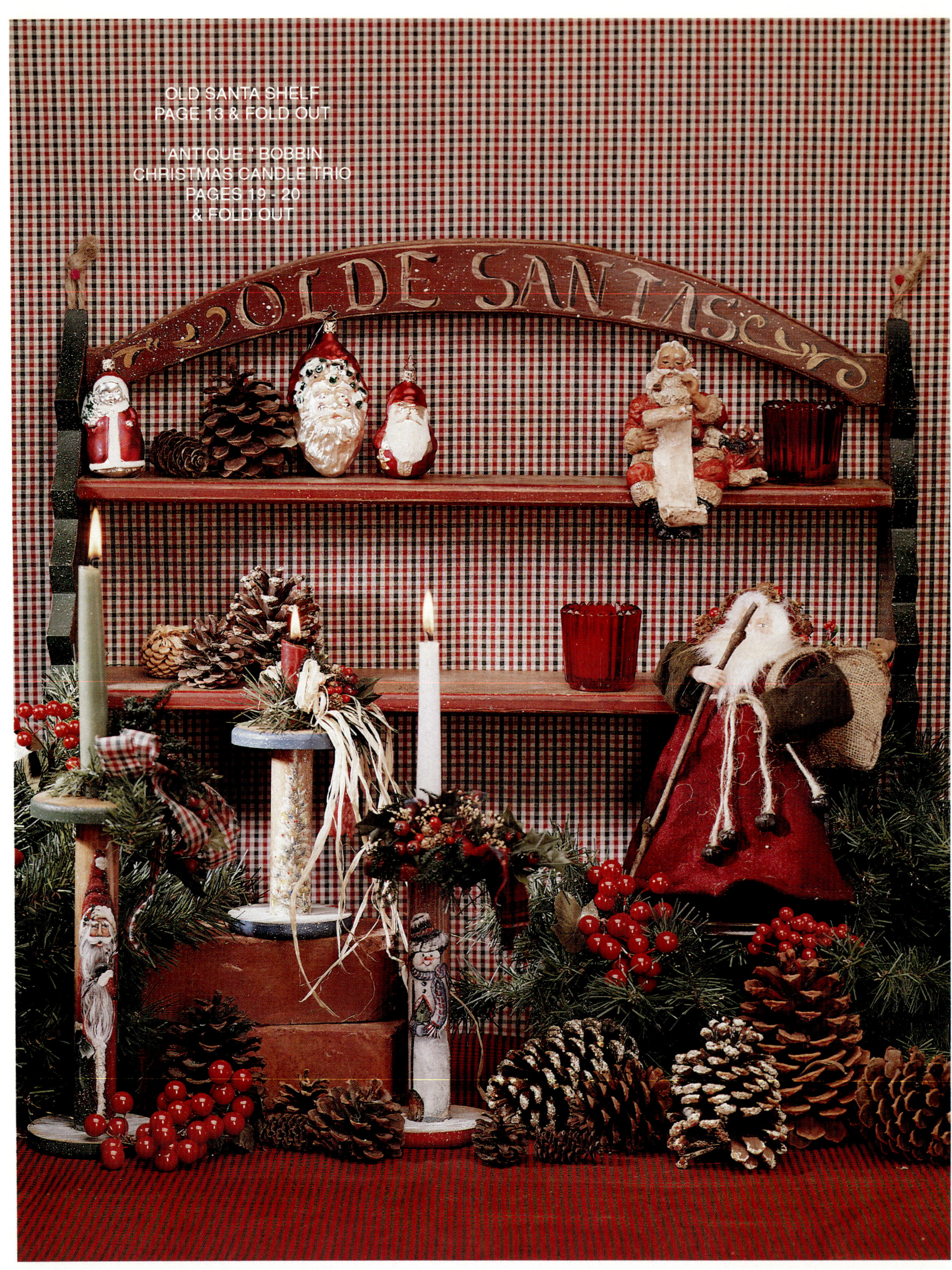

OLD SANTA SHELF
PAGE 13 & FOLD OUT

"ANTIQUE" BOBBIN
CHRISTMAS CANDLE TRIO
PAGES 19 - 20
& FOLD OUT

OLDE SANTAS

Old Santa Shelf

Being a Santa Collector Myself I'm Always Seeking Unusual Ways to Display Them.
I Hope You Like This One!!

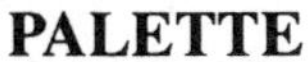

PALETTE
Cherry Royale
Southern Pine
Licorice
Taffy
Metallic Gold

BRUSHES
No. 2 Flat Shader
2 Inch Sponge Brush
No. 3 Round

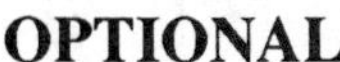

MISCELLANEOUS
Down Home Brown Antique

OPTIONAL
    A detail sander was used on this piece. It's a wonderful tool and saves much time and arm work. It is relatively inexpensive. Of course, you can simply hand sand to achieve a nice "antique" look.

INSTRUCTIONS

1. **SAND AND TACK WOOD**
   Stain with "inky" Down Home Brown and sponge brush. Let dry.

2. **TREES:** Basecoat total tree with Southern Pine. Let dry. Sand off all edges.

3. **BANNER SIGN**
   Basecoat front surface with Cherry Royale. Transfer pattern for lettering. Lettering is painted with No. 2 flat shader and Taffy. Using No. 3 round line to the left of all letters using Licorice. Gold comma stroke work is painted with No. 3 round, lined to the left with Licorice. Let dry. Sand edges.

4. Trim front of shelves with Cherry Royale. Antique all pieces with Down Home Brown.

5. **FINISH:** Varnish with water base varnish. Spatter all with old tooth brush and "inky" Taffy.

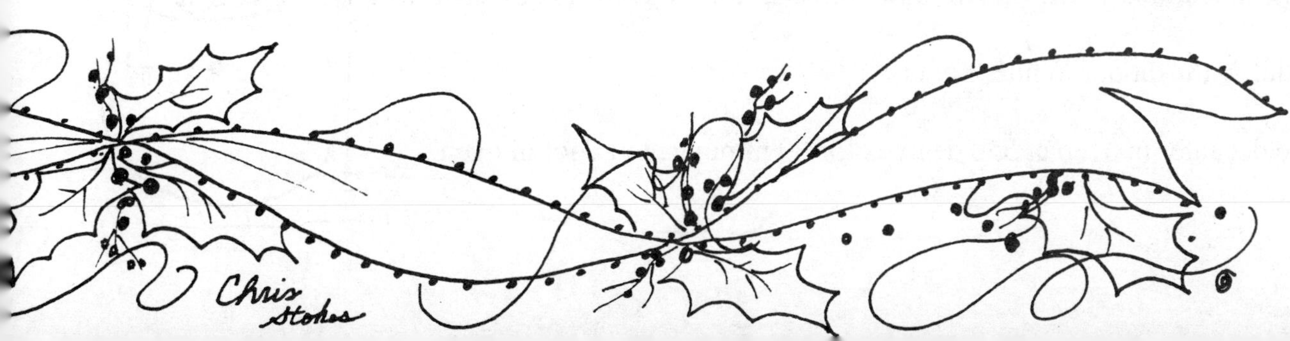

Snow Man Lotion / Soap Pump

This porcelain pump came from Viking Woodcraft and was very easy and fun to paint.

PALETTE (Apple Barrel Acrylic Gloss Enamel)

Goodnight Blue	Antique White
Real Red	Real Green
Black	Tangerine
Coffee Bean	

BRUSHES

Nos. 4 and 8 Flat Shader
No. 00 Liner

MISCELLANEOUS

Natural Sponge

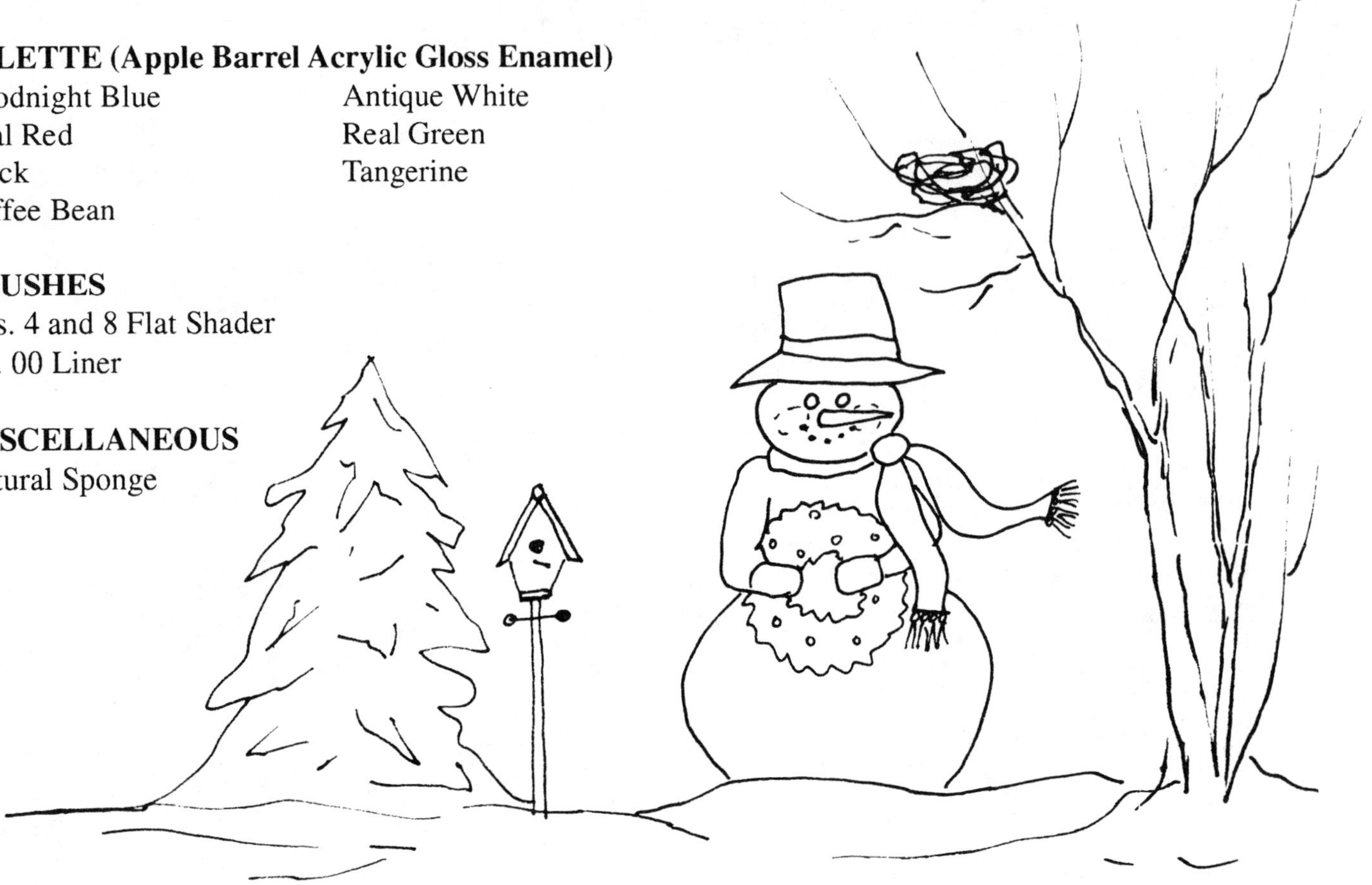

INSTRUCTIONS

1.   **WASH AND DRY DISPENSER:** Using natural sponge, sponge with doubleload of Goodnight Blue/Antique White. Let dry, transfer patterns.

2.   **SNOWMAN**
   Basecoat with No. 8 flat shade Coffee Bean.
   Cheeks: floated Real Red.
   Coal Eyes and Mouth : dotted in with Black.
   Nose is Tangerine.
   Hat is Black.
   Snow on hat and nose is Antique White.
   Wreath is pounced in the Real Green.
   Real Red berries are dotted in.
   Scarf and gloves are painted in with Real Red. Real Green stripes on scarf.
   Sideload Antique White on No. 8 flat brush and wisp snow under snowman.

3.   Spatter with Antique White. Let dry.

4.   Bake decanter in oven at 350 degrees for 30 minutes. Let cool in oven.

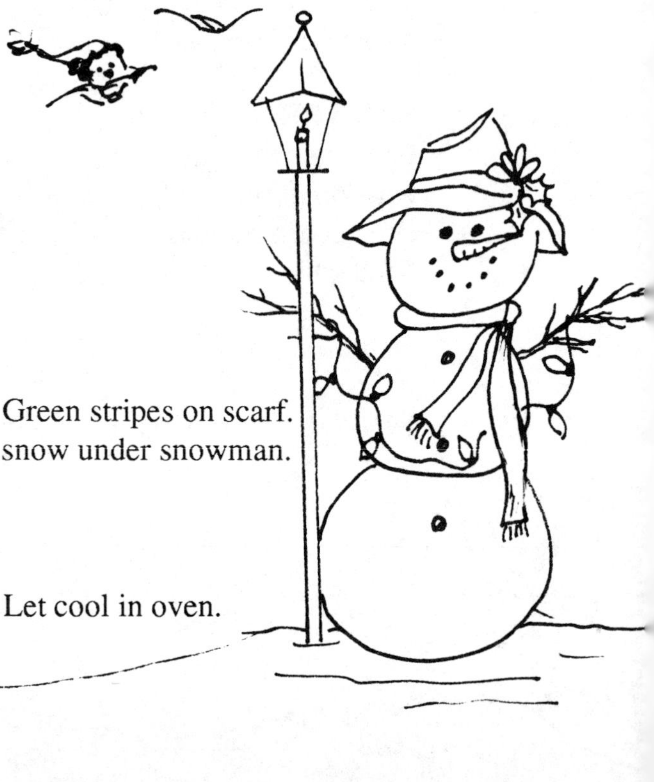

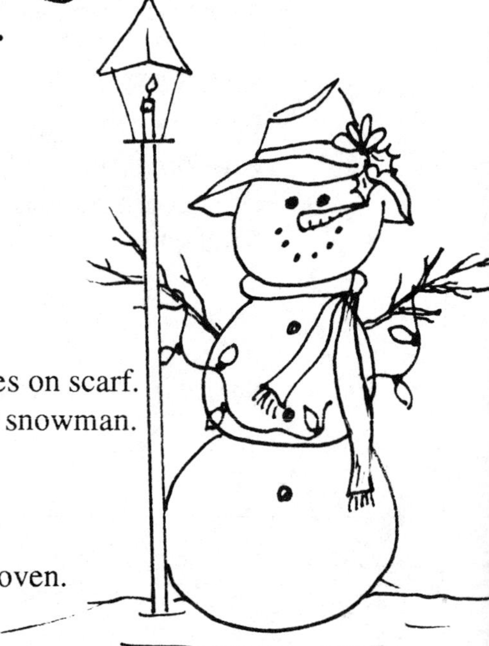

"Antique" Saint Nick Sled

*So many of you have requested more Santas for this realistic antique sled I designed.
I hope your like my Saint Nick!!!*

MATERIALS
Wooden "Antique" Sled available through The Craft Cottage.

PALETTE
Midnight	Skintone
Molasses	Apple Spice
Emerald Isle	Licorice
Brick Red	Burnt Umber
Wicker White	English Mustard
Taffy	Burnt Sienna
Metallic Gold	

BRUSHES
3/8 Inch Angler	No. 00 Liner
3/4 Inch Glaze	1/2 Inch Glaze
2 Inch Sponge Brush	Small Stencil Brush (to stipple fur)
Large Filbert Rake	No. 2 Flat (line work on flag)

MISCELLANEOUS
Water Base Varnish
Natural Sponge
Down Home Brown Antique

INSTRUCTIONS
1. **SAND AND TACK SLED:** Using sponge brush and "inky" Down Home Brown Antique, stain entire sled. Let dry. Using natural sponge, sponge front of sled with Midnight and touch of Taffy. Center area is lighter. Let dry. Transfer St. Nick pattern.

2. **SAINT NICK FACE:** Basecoat with Skintone, shade Burnt Sienna. Eye sockets are Wicker White, iris is floated in Burnt Sienna. Pupil is Licorice dot, Wicker White sparkle and Licorice lashes. Cheeks are floated with Brick Red. Deepen shading with Molasses. Lip is floated Brick Red. Highlight with Taffy.

3. **COAT:** Basecoat with Apple Spice, shade Apple Spice and touch of Midnight. Highlight is Brick Red. Highlight lighter areas (refer to photo) with Brick Red and touch of Taffy.

4. **GOWN:** Basecoat Emerald Isle, shade Midnight, highlight Emerald Isle and touch of Taffy. Stripe on bottom is Taffy and touch of English Mustard. Edge is Brick Red, highlight with Taffy.

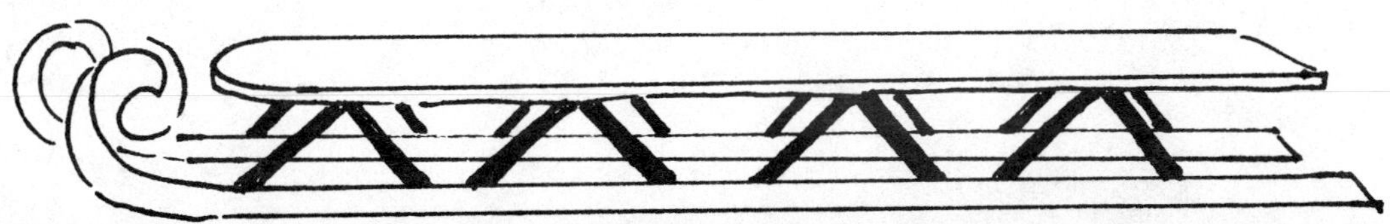

"Antique" Saint Nick Sled continued

5.   **ST. NICK SACK:** Paint English Mustard and touch of Taffy, shade with Burnt Umber. Stipple greenery in sack. Birdhouse is Taffy, shade with Burnt Umber. Paint rood Emerald Isle, highlight Taffy. Flag is totally painted with Taffy. Star area is Midnight. Stars are Taffy. Red stripes are Apple Spice, shaded with Burnt Umber. Flag pole and knob are painted English Mustard, highlight with Taffy. Twigs are painted with liner and "inky" Taffy or Burnt Umber randomly. Holly is sideloaded Emerald Isle and touch of Taffy. Berries are randomly dots of Brick Red, then Apple Spice. Cardinal is Apple Spice, highlight Brick Red, Licorice and Black.

6.   **BEARD:** Undercoat beard in Burnt Umber and touch of English Mustard on a filbert rake brush (use a sweeping dry brush method). Next dip your brush into water (with dark paint still in brush), then into more English Mustard, sweep hair and curls in. Next, leaving the previous colors in brush, add Taffy then pick up Wicker White on the liner brush and wisp fine line hairs in. Pipe in Licorice, highlight Taffy. Smoke is dry brushed in with Taffy and touch of Midnight.

7.   **ARMS AND GLOVES:** Arm is Apple Spice, shade Licorice, highlight Brick Red. Gloves are Licorice, highlight with a touch of Taffy.

8.   **FUR:** Stipple frost with Burnt Umber/English Mustard. Let dry, pounce lightly with Taffy and touch of English Mustard.

9.   **TREE:** Using angle brush, doubleloaded Midnight on short end, Emerald Isle on long end, pounce lightly to blend, hold vertically and pounce tree in. Add a touch of Taffy to long end of brush, pounce, blend together and highlight tree. Truck is Licorice, highlight with English Mustard.

10.   **LETTERING (Common Strokes):** Paint with Metallic Gold and No. 00 liner.

11.   **SNOW BANKS:** Sideload 3/4 inch glaze brush with Taffy and pull puffy hills in.

12.   **FINISHING:** Spatter with old tooth brush and "inky' Taffy. Let dry. Varnish with water base varnish. Decorate as desired - berries, greenery, a bird house, and a small red bird was used on this project.

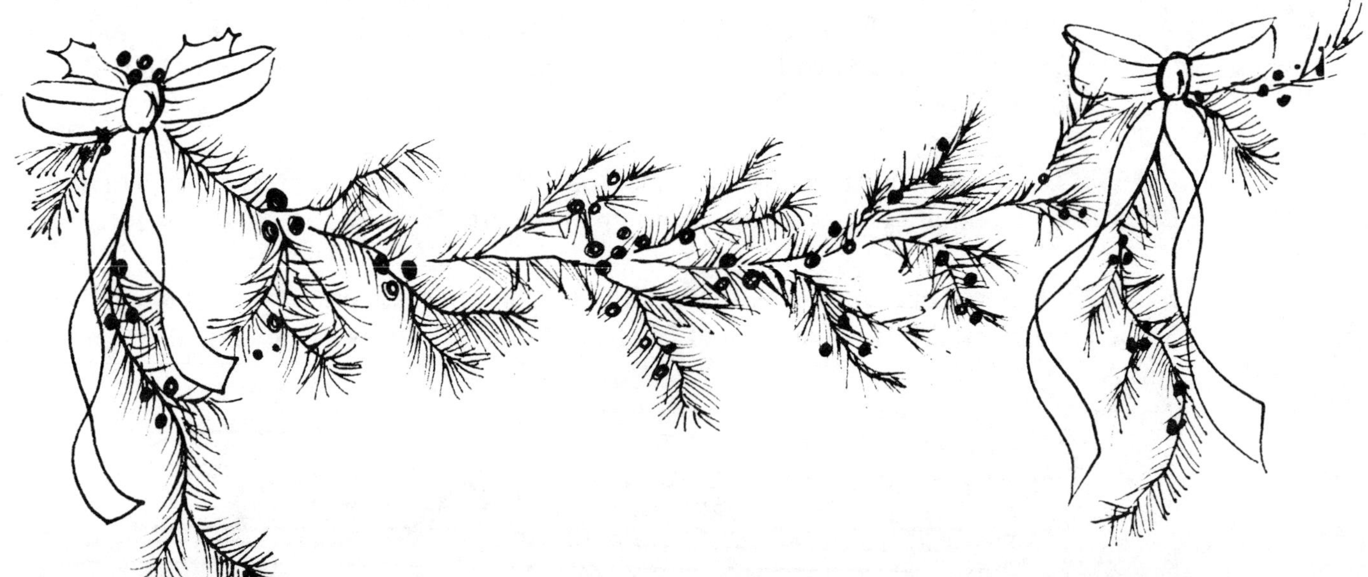

Victorian Rose Father Christmas Gourd

Another Collectible Santa
Would also be very cute painted on a sweatshirt!

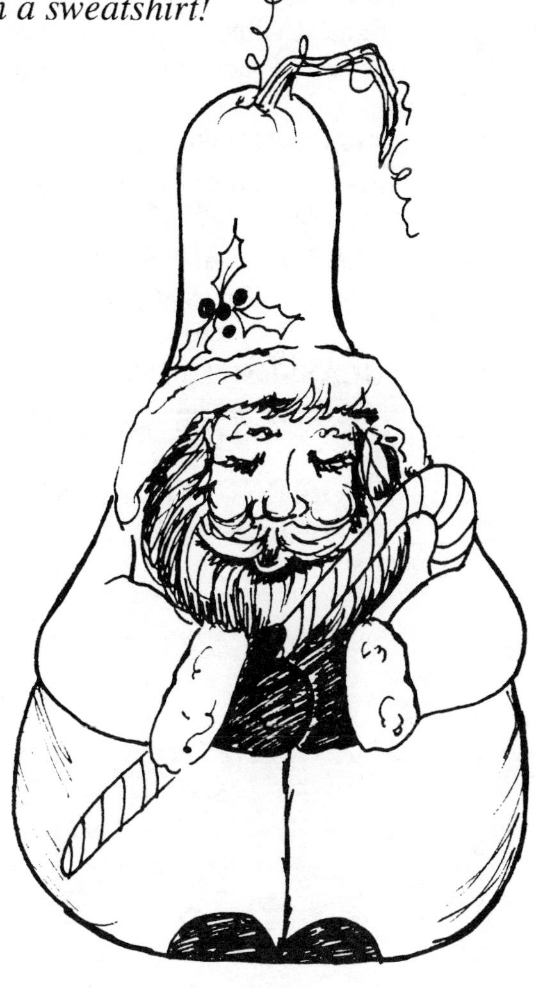

PALETTE

Almond Parfait	Moon Yellow
Emerald Isle	Burnt Carmine
Chocolate Fudge	Potpourri Rose
Portrait Dark	French Blue
Taffy	Burnt Sienna
Titanium White	Charcoal Grey
Licorice	Thunder Blue
Pure Gold	

BRUSHES

3/4 Inch Glaze (to basecoat gourd)
Nos. 2, 8 and 10 Flat
1/2 Inch Rake by La Cornelle

MATERIALS:

Large kettle gourd washed, dried and ready to paint.

MISCELLANEOUS

Wooden "Shoes" (pattern provided)

INSTRUCTIONS

1. Basecoat entire Santa with Licorice. Transfer pattern.

2. **FACE:** (See basic Santa face demo). Basecoat with Almond Parfait, shade Burnt Sienna.
    Re-shade Chocolate Fudge. Eyes: Float with Thunder Blue.

3. **GOWN:** Basecoat with Potpourri Rose, shade Burnt Carmine.

4. **ARMS:** Highlight arms and pleats in sleeves with floated French Blue.

5. **BANDING ON COAT AND HOOD:** Using No. 10 flat paint banding in with Moon Yellow.
    When dry wash over this same area with Taffy.

6. **ROSEBUDS ON BANDING:** Painted with a doubleloaded No. 2 flat with Burnt Carmine/
    Taffy. Leaves are doubleloaded Emerald Isle/Taffy. Vines are "inky" Emerald Isle. Shade
    banding with Chocolate Fudge. Outline only the edges of banding with "inky" Pure Gold
    squiggles.

7. **GLOVES:** Doubleloaded No 10 flat with Emerald Isle/Licorice.

Victorian Rose Father Christmas continued

8.   **BEARD:** Use 1/2 inch rake with very "inky" paint. Undercoat darkest value Charcoal Grey and touch of Taffy. Pick up additional Taffy for medium value. Pick up Titanium White as your lightest value. Curling and wisping as you go. Final step is liner brush Titanium White wisps of hair. Practice this technique, it's fun and easy with great results.

9.   **ROSES ON HOOD:** Doubleload No. flat with Taffy/Burnt Carmine for darkest rose. Lightest rose is Titanium White/Potpourri Rose.

10.   **HOLLY LEAVES:** Use doubleloaded No 8 flat with Emerald Isle/Taffy. Outline Pure Gold comma strokes and berries.

11.   **GLASSES:** Float bottom of glasses with scant amount of Thunder Blue. Float top of glasses Titanium White. Paint Titanium White comma on glasses. Rims are Pure Gold.

12.   **FINISHING:** Spray with Folk Art Acrylic Sealer. Hot glue little wooden "shoes" on Santa and you've got one gorgeous gourd.

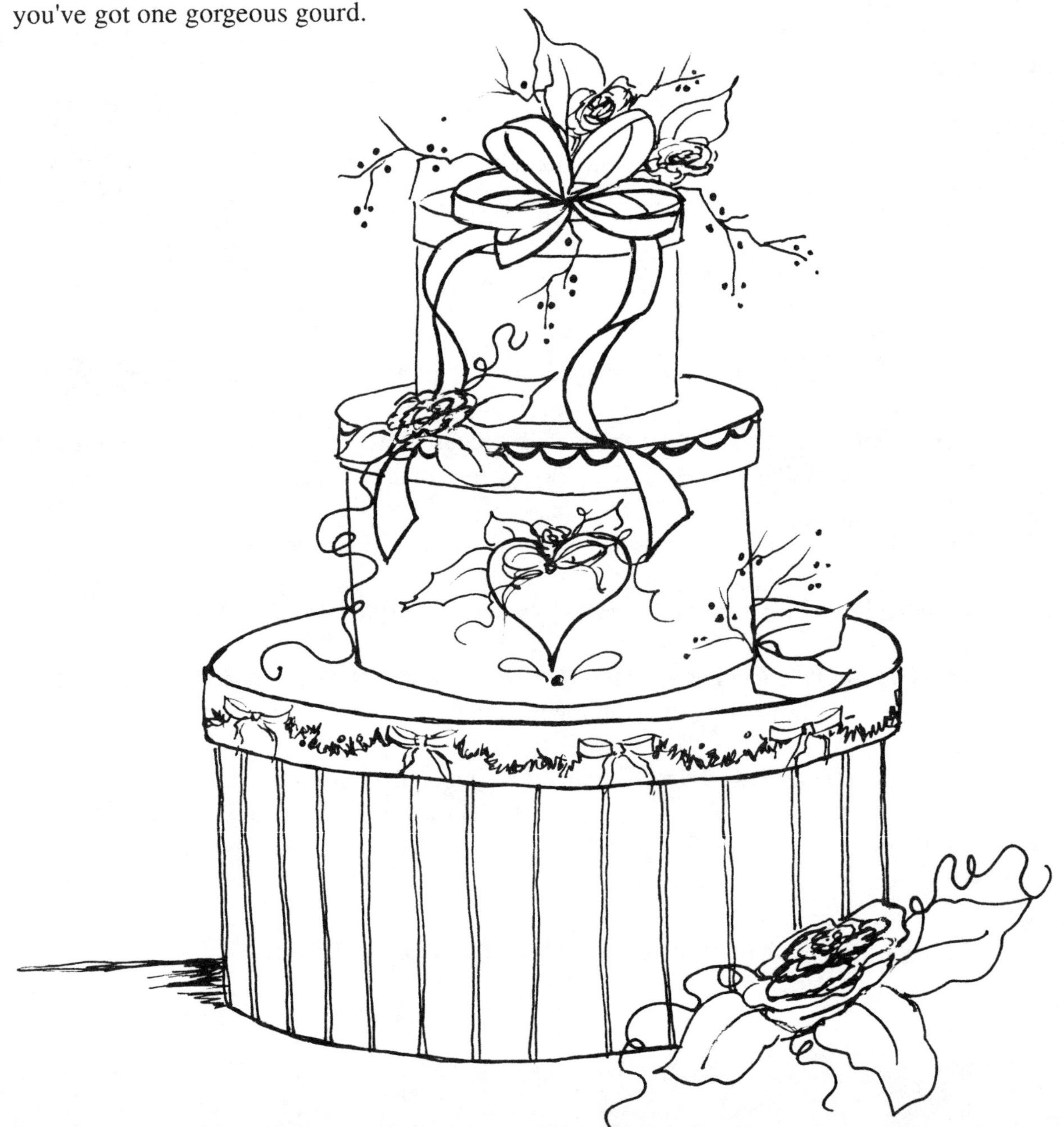

"Antique" Bobbin
Christmas Candle Trio

Old thread bobbins are very scarce now, so I designed these three...
Easy and fun to paint.

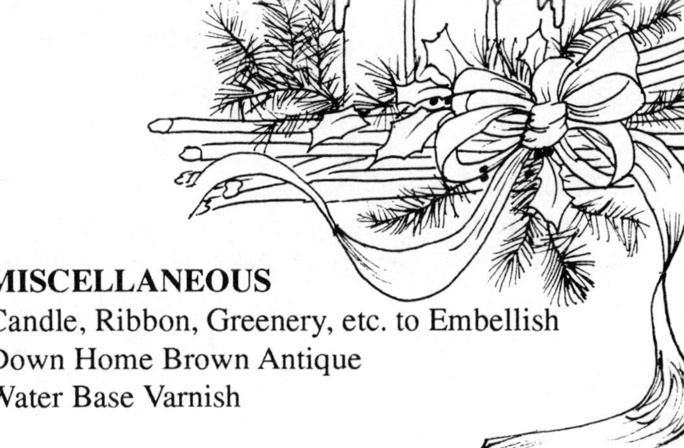

Santa Bobbin
PALETTE

Red Light	Licorice
Old Ivy	Apricot Cream
Dutch Blue	Burnt Carmine
Warm White	Blue Ribbon
Molasses	

BRUSHES
Script Liner
1/4 Inch Betty Byrd Filbert Rake
No. 8 Flat
Stylus

MISCELLANEOUS
Candle, Ribbon, Greenery, etc. to Embellish
Down Home Brown Antique
Water Base Varnish

INSTRUCTIONS

1. **SAND AND TACK WOOD:** Stain all bobbins with "inky" Down Home Brown. Let Dry. Transfer pattern.

2. **SANTA'S FACE:** Apricot Cream, shade Molasses. Cheeks are floated with Red Light. Eyes are Blue Ribbon, Licorice pupil and lashes.

3. **HAT AND COAT:** Basecoat Red Light, shade Burnt Carmine. Highlight Red Light and touch of Warm White.

4. **BEARD:** Loosely undercoat Dutch Blue and touch of Licorice. Wipe out brush, add touch of water and Warm White and stroke hair in. Add liner brush strokes of Warm White.

5. **GLOVES:** Licorice, highlight Warm White.

6. **BAG:** Old Ivy, highlight Warm White, shade Burnt Carmine. Patches are Blue Ribbon; Red Light - "stitched" with "inky" Licorice,

7. **FUR:** Stipple with Warm White, shade Molasses.

8. **HOLLY AND TWIG IN HAND:** Old Ivy. Red Light and Burnt Carmine berries dotted with stylus. Twigs are inky Licorice.

9. **FINISH:** Double load Dutch Blue/Warm White on brush and "swish" snow under Santa. Trim bobbin with Old Ivy. Varnish with water base varnish. Spatter with Warm White and decorate.

 ## <u>Snowman Bobbin</u>

PALETTE

Dutch Blue
Blue Ribbon
Licorice
Red Orange

Wicker White
English Mustard
Pure Pigment Burnt Umber

BRUSHES

1/2 Inch Folk Art Stencil
Script Liner
No. 8 Flat

MISCELLANEOUS

Water Base Varnish
Down Home Brown Antique (to stain bobbin)
Candle, Ribbon, Etc., to embellish candle holder.

1. **SNOWMAN:** Stipple in using doubleloaded stencil brush Wicker White/Dutch Blue. Let dry, shade with Dutch blue, float cheeks in with Red Light.
CARROT NOSE: Red Orange. Eyes are dotted with Licorice, Wicker White sparkle. Red Light smile. Hat is Licorice, highlight Wicker White. Add heavy Wicker White snow.

2. **SCARF:** Blue Ribbon, stripes are Old Ivy, Red Light, Wicker White.
GLOVES: Blue Ribbon, highlight Wicker White.

3. **BIRDHOUSE:** Roof is Red Light, shade Licorice. Walls are Old Ivy wash, shade Licorice.

4. **BROOM:** Handle is English Mustard, shade Burnt Umber, repeat for straw. Red Light stitching. Trim with Red Light.

5. **FINISH:** Varnish with water base varnish. Spatter with Warm White and decorate.

<u>Christmas Tree Bobbin</u>

PALETTE

Blue Ribbon
Red Light
Butter Cream

Permanent Pigment Yellow Medium
Southern Pine
Antique Gold

BRUSHES

1/2 Inch Angler
Stylus

Script Liner
No. 4 Flat

1. **TREE:** Doubleload angle brush with Butter Cream on long end/Southern Pine on short end. Pounce lightly then stipple in holding angler brush vertically.

2. **CANDLES:** Float Yellow Medium "halo" around flame, candles are painted with liner brush and Butter Cream. Flame is Red Light/Yellow Medium mix. Antique Gold at base of each candle.

3. **STYLUS DOTS:** Using Blue Ribbon, Red Light finishes decorating this little tree.

4. **FINISH:** Trim with Blue Ribbon and flat blue and white mixes for snow on base. Varnish with water base varnish and spatter with Warm White and decorate.

Star Santa Tree Topper

He Also Looks Very Cute in His Stand.
The Buttons Add a Real Down Home Feeling.

PALETTE

Apple Spice
Southern Pine
Molasses
Licorice
Skintone
Azure Blue

Old Ivy
Harvest Gold
Christmas Red
Wicker White
Taffy

BRUSHES

Nos. 4 and 8 Flats
Liner
2 Inch Sponge Brush
Large Filbert Rake

INSTRUCTIONS

1. **SAND AND TACK WOOD** (Use sponge brush)
   Stain with "inky" Down Home Brown Antique. Let dry. Paint front surface of Santa with Apple Spice. Front surface of star is painted Harvest Gold. Shade star with Molasses. Transfer necessary pattern.

2. **FACE:** Basecoat Skintone, shade Molasses. Basecoat eye socket Wicker White. Iris is floated Azure Blue, Licorice pupil. Eyelashes are "inky" Licorice. Sparkle is Wicker White. Cheeks are floated in Christmas Red. Lips are floated in Apple Spice.

3. **SANTA'S OUTFIT:** Using No. 4 flat, paint a wash stripe of Taffy and pull stripe in. Cross in opposite direction with Old Ivy, wash stripe. Use liner and Taffy for lighter lines. Darker green squares are Southern Pine (refer to photo for guidance). Shade with Licorice.

4. **GLOVES AND BOOTS:** Gloves are painted Licorice. Boots are painted Harvest Gold, shade with Molasses. Laces are Licorice, highlight Licorice tips of boots with Taffy.

5. **BEARD AND BROWS:** Using large filbert rake brush and "inky" Taffy and Licorice wisp beard in - pick up more Taffy as you wisp more hair in. Finally pick up "inky" Wicker White with liner and pull fine hairs.

6. Stipple fur in with Taffy and touch of Licorice. Holly in hat is Southern Pine. Berries are dotted in using Christmas Red.

7. **FINISH**
   Varnish with water base varnish. Glue wire with star attached and buttons in hand. Burlap sack (made from a scrap of burlap) is stuffed with greenery, cinnamon sticks and other goodies attached by jute and glued to Santa's leg. The base that holds him when he's not used as a tree topper is Old Ivy trimmed in Apple Spice. Wrap jute belt around waist. Pipe cleaner is stapled on back to attach to tree.

Noah's Ark Santa Stocking

PALETTE

Old Ivy	Pure Pigment Titanium White
Moon Yellow	Chocolate Fudge
Harvest Gold	Cherry Royale
Licorice	Almond Parfait
Blue Ribbon	Pure Pigment Burnt Sienna

BRUSHES

Liner	1/4 Inch Filbert Rake
No. 10 Flat Shader	1/2 Inch Stencil Brush (To stencil fur on cuff of stocking)
Small Old Scruffy Brush	2 Inch Sponge Brush
No. 4 Flat Shader	1/2 Inch Angler

MISCELLANEOUS

Down Home Brown Antique
Water Base Varnish

INSTRUCTIONS

1. **SAND AND TACK WOOD**
   Using 2 inch sponge brush and "inky" Down Home Brown Antique, stain entire piece. Let dry. Paint surface only with one coat of Moon Yellow. Let dry. Sand with paper sack. Transfer pattern.

2. **SANTA**
   Face: Basecoat Almond Parfait, shade Burnt Sienna.
   Eyes: Basecoat socket Titanium White. Iris is Blue ribbon, pupil Licorice. Chocolate Fudge eyelashes.
   Cheeks: Floated in with Cherry Royale.
   Beard: The beard is painted in after the coat is painted using 1/4 inch filbert rake and "inky" Chocolate Fudge. Next pick up Titanium White, final wisps are pulled in with liner brush and Titanium White.
   Gloves: Licorice. Belt is Chocolate Fudge.

3. **PATCHWORK COAT**
   Patches are randomly "washed" with No. 4 flat shader using Blue Ribbon, Harvest Gold, Cherry Royal and Old Ivy. "Inky" stitches of Chocolate Fudge.

4. **NOAH'S ARK**
   Boat: Harvest Gold, shade Chocolate Fudge.
   House Part: Blue Ribbon, shade Licorice. Windows and doors are Licorice. Outline with "inky" Titanium White. Roof is Cherry Royale.

5. **SANTA'S BAG AND HAT:** "Wash" with Cherry Royale, shade with Cherry Royale.

6.   **TREE:** Using angler brush double loaded with Old Ivy/Licorice pounce tree in.

7.   **MERRY CHRISTMAS BANNER:** Pole is Licorice highlighted Moon Yellow and touch of Titanium White. Flag is Old Ivy. Lettering is "inky" Titanium White.

8.   **FUR:** Stipple in using Titanium White. Let dry. Shade with Chocolate Fudge.

9.   **STOCKING:** Shade with Chocolate Fudge.

10.   **RANDOM SNOW FLAKES:** Use Titanium White, using handle end of brush then pull out spikes using brush end of liner. Dot some tips.

11.   **HEEL:** Washed in with Old Ivy "stitch" with "inky" Chocolate Fudge. Toe is "inky" Cherry Royale stitched in with Chocolate Fudge.

12.   **FUR CUFF:** Using large stencil brush, stipple using Chocolate Fudge. Stipple over this with heavy Titanium White. Let dry.

13.   **FINISH:** Varnish with water base varnish. Spatter with Titanium White snow. Decorate with greenery and ark animals, etc.

Moon Santa Clock

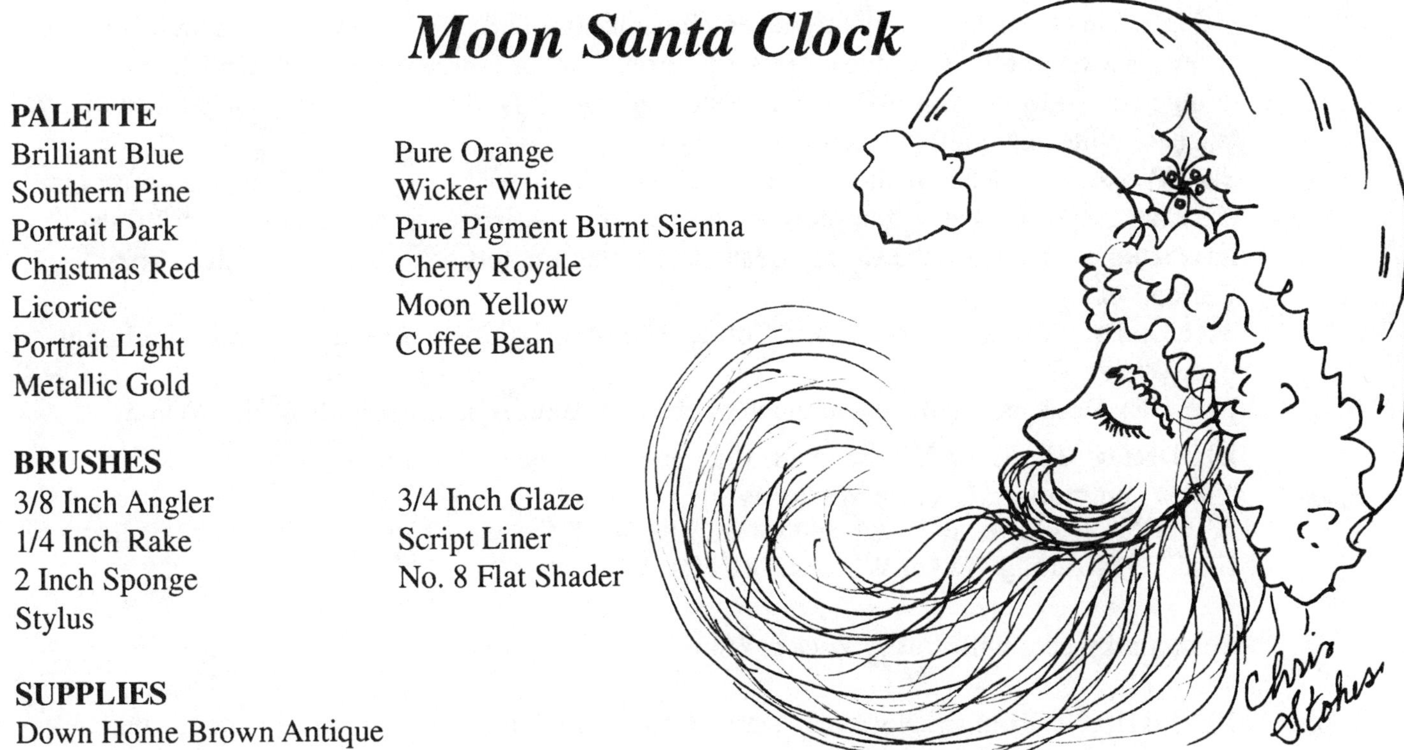

PALETTE

Brilliant Blue
Southern Pine
Portrait Dark
Christmas Red
Licorice
Portrait Light
Metallic Gold

Pure Orange
Wicker White
Pure Pigment Burnt Sienna
Cherry Royale
Moon Yellow
Coffee Bean

BRUSHES

3/8 Inch Angler
1/4 Inch Rake
2 Inch Sponge
Stylus

3/4 Inch Glaze
Script Liner
No. 8 Flat Shader

SUPPLIES

Down Home Brown Antique
Water Base Varnish
Wooden Clock available through Viking Wood Crafts, many Craft Suppliers and of course The Craft Cottage.

Moon Santa Clock

INSTRUCTIONS

1. **SAND AND TACK WOOD**
   With sponge brush stain all pieces with Down Home Brown Antique. Let dry. Paint surface of Clock face with Moon Yellow. Front of clock insert, base and sides are painted Brilliant Blue. Let dry. Transfer pattern.

2. **MOON SANTA**
   FACE: Basecoat Portrait Light, shade with Portrait Dark, re-shade Burnt Sienna.
   EYE SOCKETS: Wicker White, float Brilliant Blue iris; Licorice pupil; Coffee Bean lashes. Linework (wrinkles, etc.) are "inky" Coffee Bean. Highlight face by dry brushing with Wicker White.
   BEARD: Painted with 1/4 inch rake and "inky" Coffee Bean and touch of Brilliant Blue (make them wispy). Pick up Moon Yellow and Wicker White, wisp this in. Use liner brush fully loaded with Wicker White and pull heavy wisps in.
   CHEEKS : Floated Christmas Red. Float around total perimeter of clock face with Coffee Brown.

3. **SANTA HAT AND FUR**
   Wash hat using 3/4 inch glaze brush with Christmas Red, shade Cherry Royale.
   FUR: Stipple first with Moon Yellow and Coffee Bean. Let dry. Re-stipple with Wicker White. Holly is floated in with Southern Pine. Add a touch of Wicker White for highlights. Cherry Royale, Christmas Red and Wicker White berries dotted with stylus for holly berries.

4. **SNOWMAN SCENE**
   Using 3/4 inch glaze brush, float Wicker White background hills in. Using angle brush pounce "inky" Wicker White trees in background. Front Christmas tree is pounced in using a double loaded Moon Yellow/Southern Pine angle brush held vertically. Pick up a touch of Wicker White and highlight as needed.
   SNOWMAN is Wicker White, shade with a touch of Licorice and Brilliant Blue. Ear muffs are Christmas Red, Wicker White snow on top. Scarf is Christmas Red, shade Licorice. Carrot nose is Pure Orange, shade Coffee Bean. Coal eyes are dots of Licorice. Mouth is "inky" Coffee Bean.
   TREE: Paint using liner brush and Coffee Bean, highlight with Moon Yellow. Re-highlight with Wicker White.
   FENCE: Posts are Licorice and touch of Brilliant Blue. Highlight with Wicker White.
   BIRDHOUSE: Moon Yellow, shade Coffee Bean. The roof and base are Southern Pine. "Snow" on roof and base are Wicker White.
   PATHWAY is "swished" back and forth using No. 8 flat and Licorice and touch of Brilliant Blue. Float strong Wicker White snowdrifts in.

5. Spatter all pieces with "inky" Wicker White.

6. **FINISHING:** Paint small wooden stars Metallic Gold to use as numbers and paint similar gold stars on sides of clock. Varnish with water base varnish.

Frosty Junior
with his Lightpost and Tree

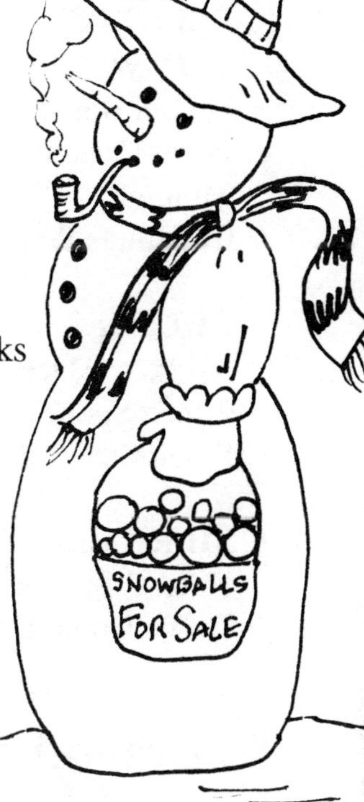

PALETTE (for all pieces)

Burnt Carmine
Autumn Leaves
Cherry Royale
Vanilla Cream
Licorice
Azure Blue
School Bus Yellow
Old Ivy

Midnight
Christmas Red
Evergreen
Country Twill
Coffee Bean
Molasses
Burnt Sienna

BRUSHES

Liner
2 Inch Sponge Brush
No. 10 Flat Shader
Stylus
3/4 Inch Flat Glaze
Small Stencil Brush for Cheeks

MISCELLANEOUS

Down Home Brown Antique
Natural Sponge

INSTRUCTIONS

1. **SAND AND TACK ALL WOOD PIECES**
   "Stain" with "inky" Down Home Brown Antique and sponge/brush. Let dry.

2. **FROSTY JUNIOR**
   Using sponge brush ,paint front surface with Country Twill. Let dry. Sand with paper sack.
   Using a damp natural sponge, pounce into Vanilla Cream and pounce on surface of Frosty. Let
   dry.
   Cheeks: Are dry brushed in using Christmas Red. Mouth is Cherry Royale.
   Eyes: Are Licorice, highlight Azure Blue.
   Carrot Nose is Autumn Leaves shade Coffee Bean and touch of Licorice. Shade frosty with
   Country Twill.
   Hat is painted in Licorice, highlight with 3/4 inch glaze brush and a touch of Azure Blue. Re-
   highlight with Vanilla Cream. Band is painted in using a double load of Cherry Royal/Autumn
   Leaves.
   Vest is Christmas Red, shade with Cherry Royale.
   Collar and Buttons are Evergreen, highlight Vanilla Cream. "Stitch" with cherry Royale.
   Tiny bow is painted in using liner brush and "inky" Vanilla Cream. Three dot-dots on vest are
   Vanilla Cream.
   Gingerbread Cookie is Country Twill, shade Burnt Sienna. Licorice raisin eyes. Cherry
   Royale nose and mouth. Outline in "inky" icing of Vanilla Cream.
   Candy Canes - Vanilla Cream, Cherry Royale stripes, shade Coffee Bean, Vanilla Cream high
   light.
   Tassels on Vest dots of Cherry Royale and Evergreen dotted with handle end of liner. Then pull
   tassel out of the wet dot with brush end of liner.

3. **LIGHT POST**
   Pole is painted Licorice. Front surface of lamp is painted School Bus Yellow. Shade lighted
   area with Burnt Sienna. Candle is painted Vanilla Cream. Wax drips are painted with double
   loaded brush. (Vanilla Cream/Azure Blue) tiny "U" strokes. Black metal area of lamp is
   Licorice. Ball on top is Metallic Gold.

Frosty Junior's Christmas Tree

PALETTE

Old Ivy	Tapioca
School Bus Yellow	Burnt Sienna
Burnt Carmine	Azure Blue
Midnight	Metallic Gold
Christmas Red	

BRUSHES

3/4 Inch Glaze
2 Inch Sponge Brush to basecoat
Small Stencil Brush to dry brush highlight

MISCELLANEOUS

Natural Sponge
Down Home Brown Antique

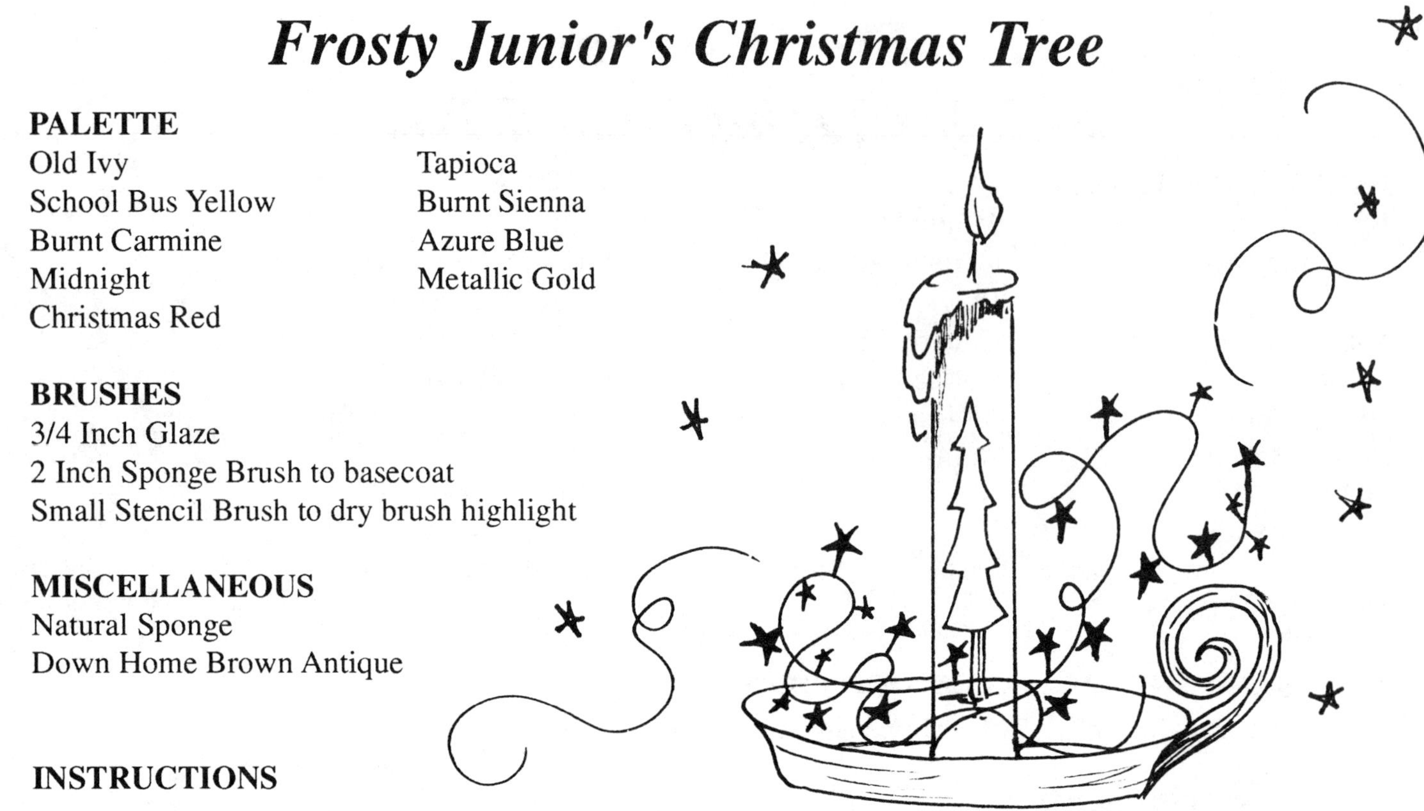

INSTRUCTIONS

1. Tree is already "stained" with down Home Brown Antique as per previous instructions. Basecoat front only with Old Ivy. Let dry. Using natural sponge double loaded Tapioca/Old Ivy, pounce snow on tree (refer to photo).

2. **GLASS BALLS**
   Blue - Basecoat Azure Blue, shade Midnight, highlight by dry brushing with Tapioca.
   Yellow - Basecoat School Bus Yellow, shade Burnt Sienna, highlight Tapioca.
   Red - Basecoat Christmas Red, shade Burnt Carmine, highlight Tapioca.

3. **FINISH**
   Varnish with water base varnish. Apply Snow Tex to surface (refer to photo for placement). Spatter with Snow Tex. Use a single electric lamp to place in lamp post. Plug in and enjoy.

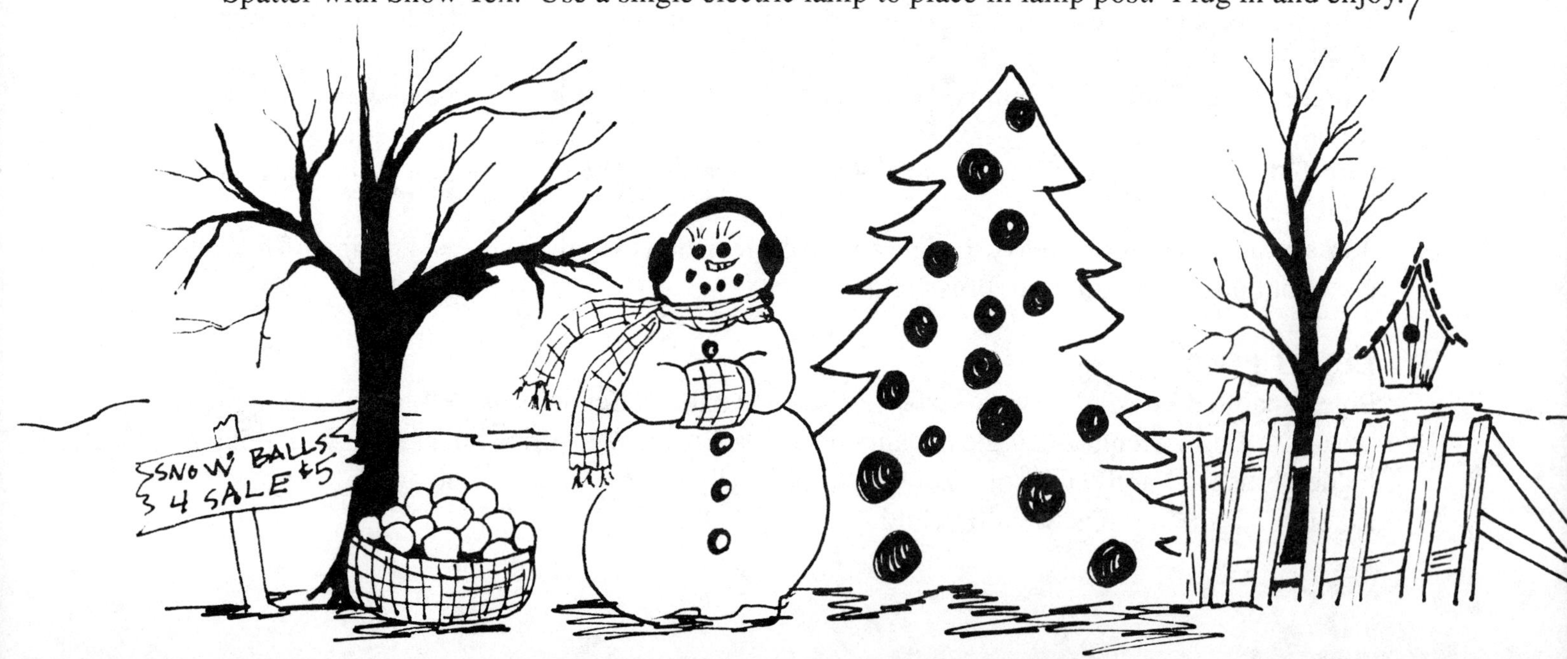

Star Santa Garland

This little Santa can also be used individually for ornaments, pins and earrings, package decorations or to wrap around a wreath. Use your imagination and have fun.

PALETTE

Skintone	Harvest Gold
Old Ivy	Apple Spice
Licorice	Wicker White
Christmas Red	Molasses
Liberty Blue	Metallic Gold
Taffy	

BRUSHES

1/4 Inch Rake
No. 8 Flat
Liner

MISCELLANEOUS

Water Base Varnish
Wired Stars to connect Santas
An assortment of buttons

INSTRUCTIONS

1. **SAND AND TACK WOOD (all pieces)**
   Stain with "inky" Down Home Antique.

2. **RED SANTA**
   Basecoat front surface with Apple Spice, shade Licorice. Belt is Licorice. Buckle is Metallic Gold.
   ALL FACES are painted Skintone, shade Molasses. Cheeks floated in with Christmas Red. Eyes are Azure Blue iris, Licorice pupil. "Inky" Licorice lashes.
   ALL BEARDS (rake brush) are undercoated with "inky" Licorice plus Taffy. Pick up more Taffy and wisp in. Use liner and wisp in Wicker White.
   ALL GLOVES are double loaded Licorice/Taffy. Shoes on Red Santa are Licorice. Dot of Metallic Gold on tip of toe.
   ALL FURS stippled in using Taffy plus Wicker White.

   GOLD SANTA
   Basecoat Harvest Gold, shade Molasses. Vest is Liberty Blue, Christmas Red outlines vest.

   GREEN SANTA
   Basecoat Old Ivy, shade Licorice. Boots are Licorice, Metallic Gold tips, Licorice belt.

3. **FINISH**
   Varnish with water base varnish. Attach each using wired gold star garland. Wrap around a small twig tree as is or paint more Santas and cover your larger tree. I added Apple and Holly picks and Baby's Breath. Now top this with Star Santa Tree Topper and place on your hearth with small packages around it or even add lights and decorate that special area.

Cookies for Santa Bear Wreath Plate

*A good beginner piece using Apple Barrel Acrylic Gloss Enamel, painted
on an inexpensive white ceramic plate.*

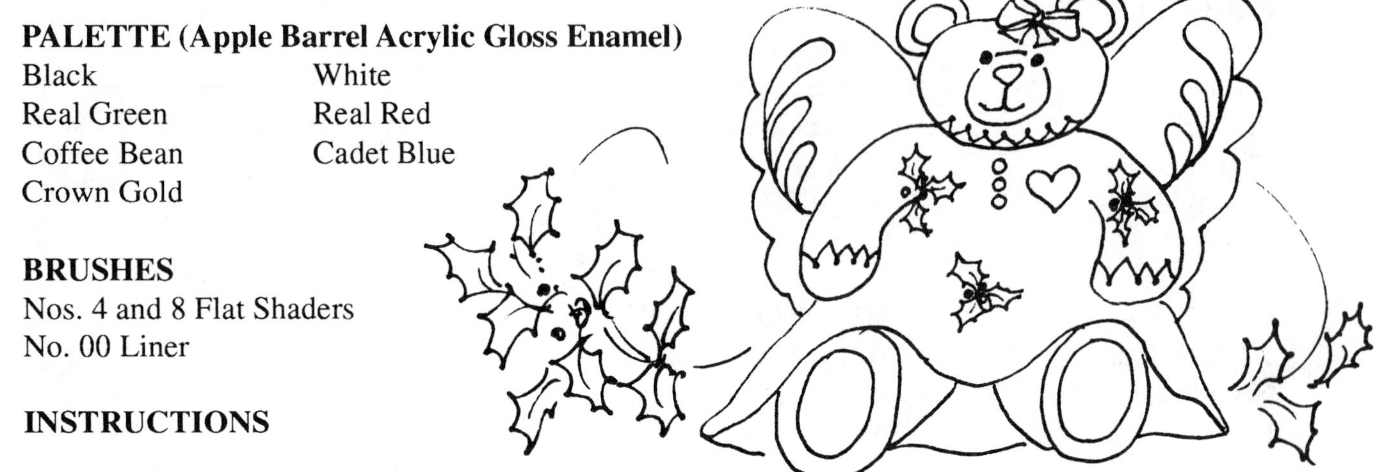

PALETTE (Apple Barrel Acrylic Gloss Enamel)

Black	White
Real Green	Real Red
Coffee Bean	Cadet Blue
Crown Gold	

BRUSHES

Nos. 4 and 8 Flat Shaders
No. 00 Liner

INSTRUCTIONS

1. **PREPARATION:** Wash plate in hot soapy water. Rinse well and dry. Transfer pattern with graphite paper.

2. **WREATH:** Form grapevine wreath using Crown Gold and #00 liner, two to three intertwined vines, then add Coffee Bean vines. Using No. 4 flat paint ribbon and bow with Real Red.

3. **BEAR:** Basecoat bear Crown Gold, shade Coffee Bean. Highlight with a touch of White. Stitching is Black. Bow on bear is doubleloaded liner touched in Cadet Blue and White. Eyes and nose are Black. Candy cane in hand is White, Real Red stripes.

4. **HOLLY AND BERRIES:** Using No. 4 flat float Real Green Holly in. Using handle end of brush dot Real Red berries and Real Red comma strokes.

5. **LETTERING:** Using No. 00 liner and Real Red outline to the right with Real Green.

6. Spatter plate with Real Green. Let dry 24 hours.

7. Bake in oven at 350 degrees for 30 minutes. Let cool in oven.

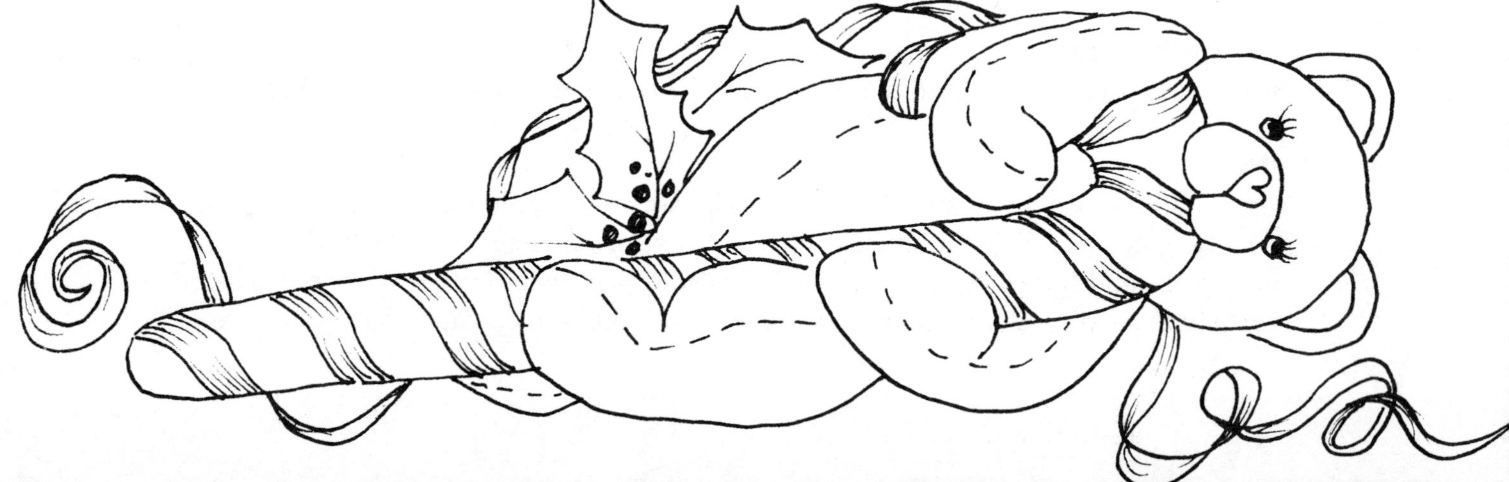

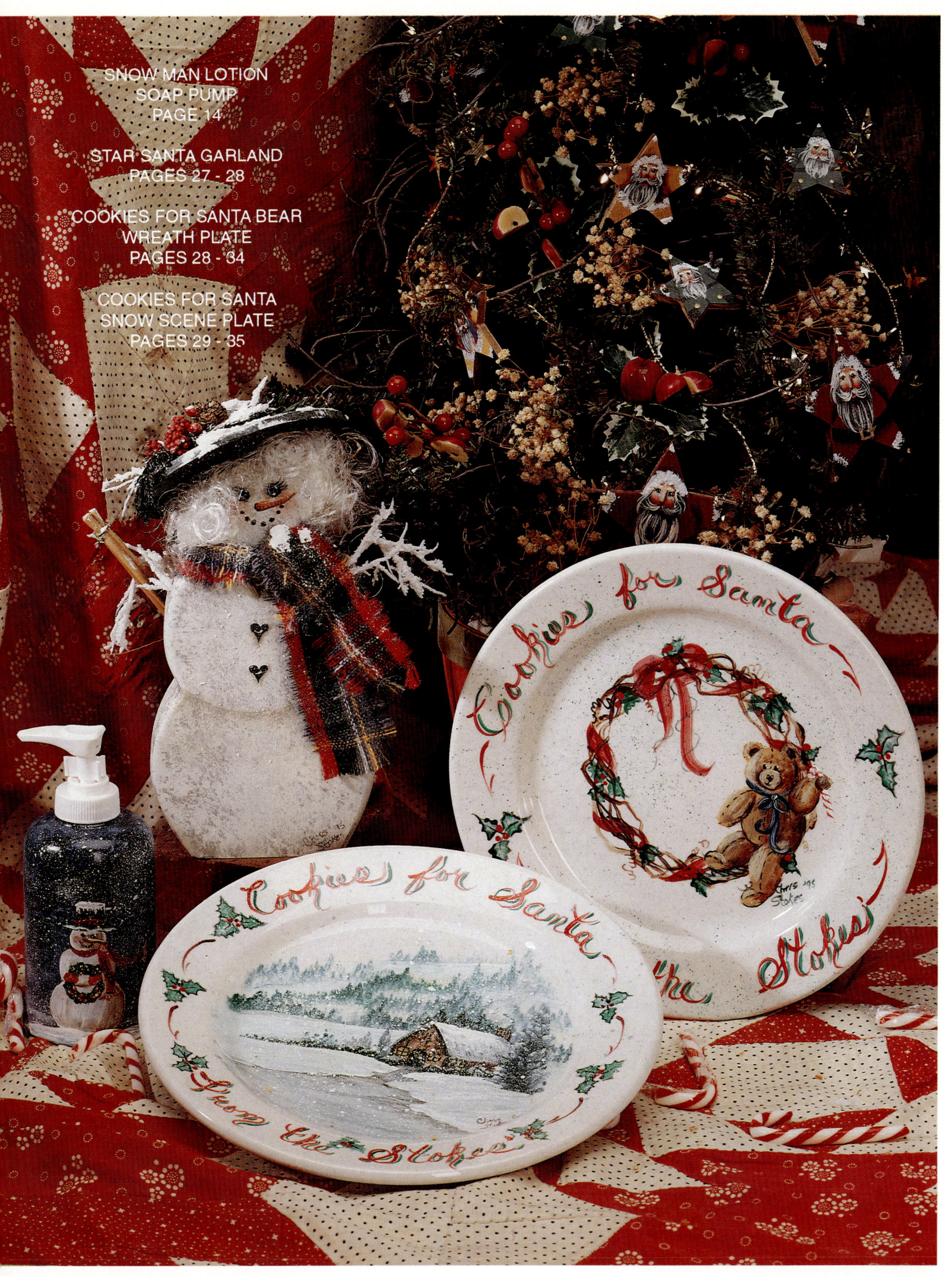

SNOW MAN LOTION
SOAP PUMP
PAGE 14

STAR SANTA GARLAND
PAGES 27 - 28

COOKIES FOR SANTA BEAR
WREATH PLATE
PAGES 28 - 34

COOKIES FOR SANTA
SNOW SCENE PLATE
PAGES 29 - 35

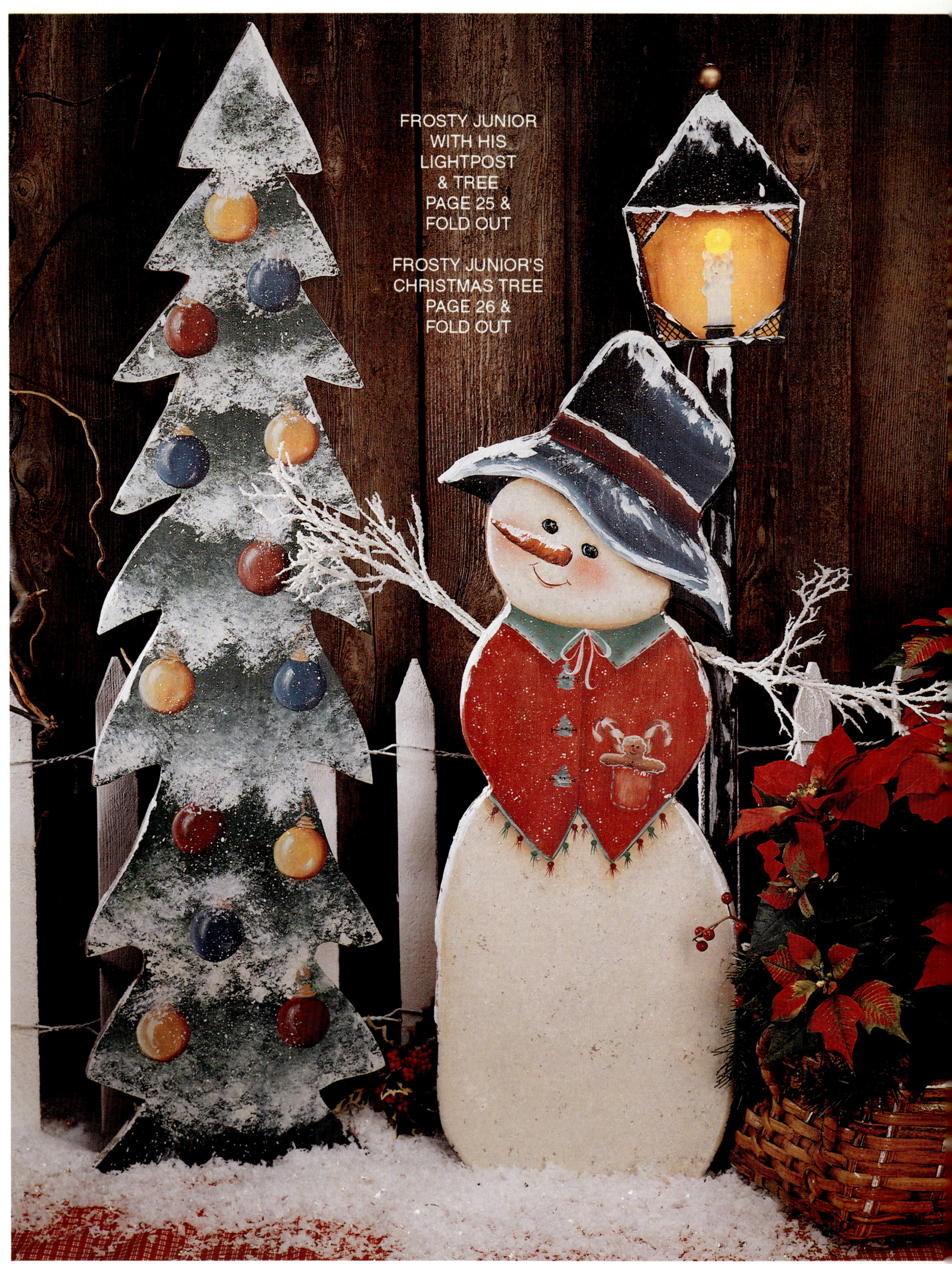

FROSTY JUNIOR
WITH HIS
LIGHTPOST
& TREE
PAGE 25 &
FOLD OUT

FROSTY JUNIOR'S
CHRISTMAS TREE
PAGE 26 &
FOLD OUT

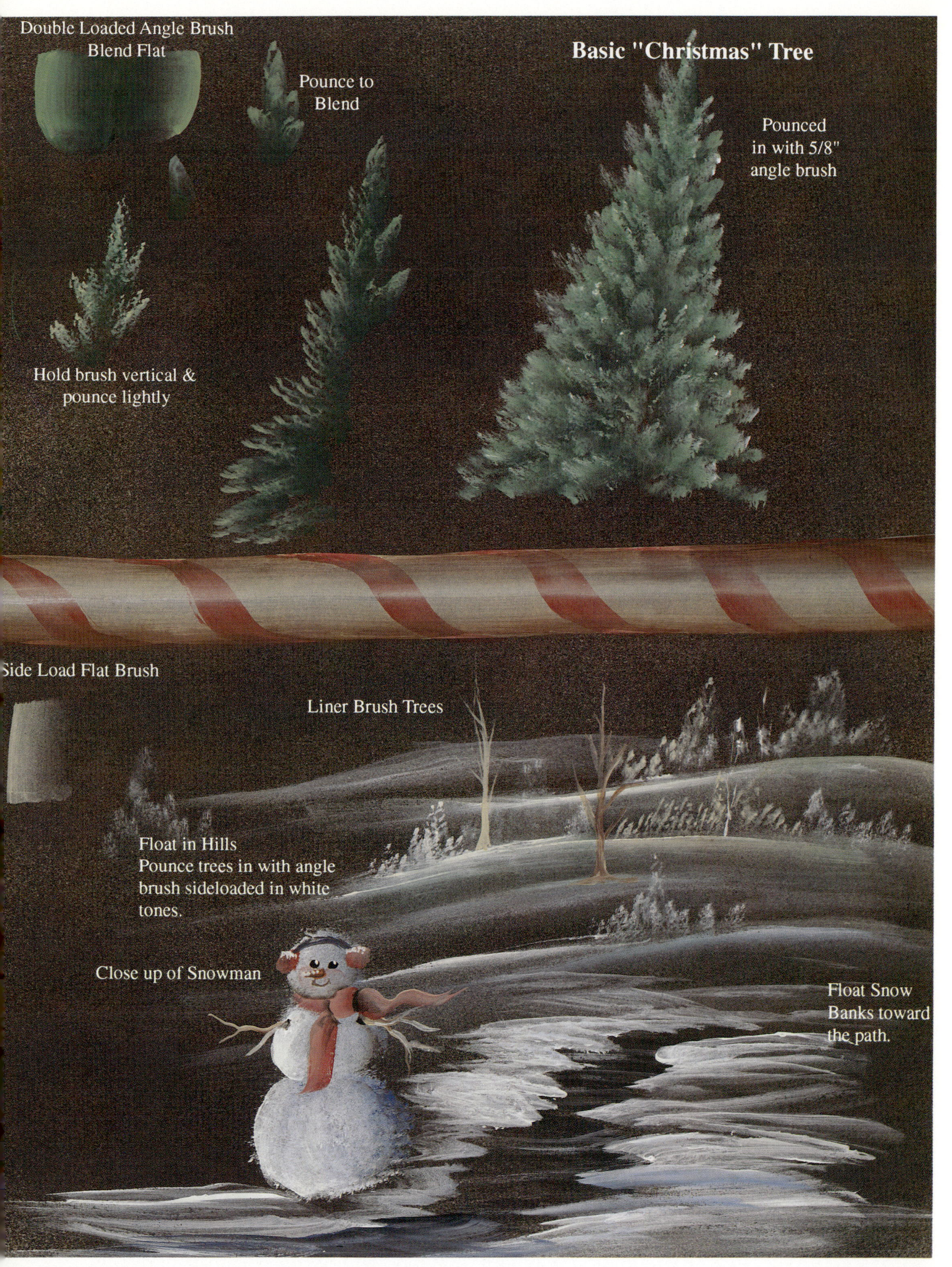

Double Loaded Angle Brush
Blend Flat
Pounce to
Blend
Basic "Christmas" Tree
Pounced
in with 5/8"
angle brush
Hold brush vertical &
pounce lightly
Side Load Flat Brush
Liner Brush Trees
Float in Hills
Pounce trees in with angle
brush sideloaded in white
tones.
Close up of Snowman
Float Snow
Banks toward
the path.

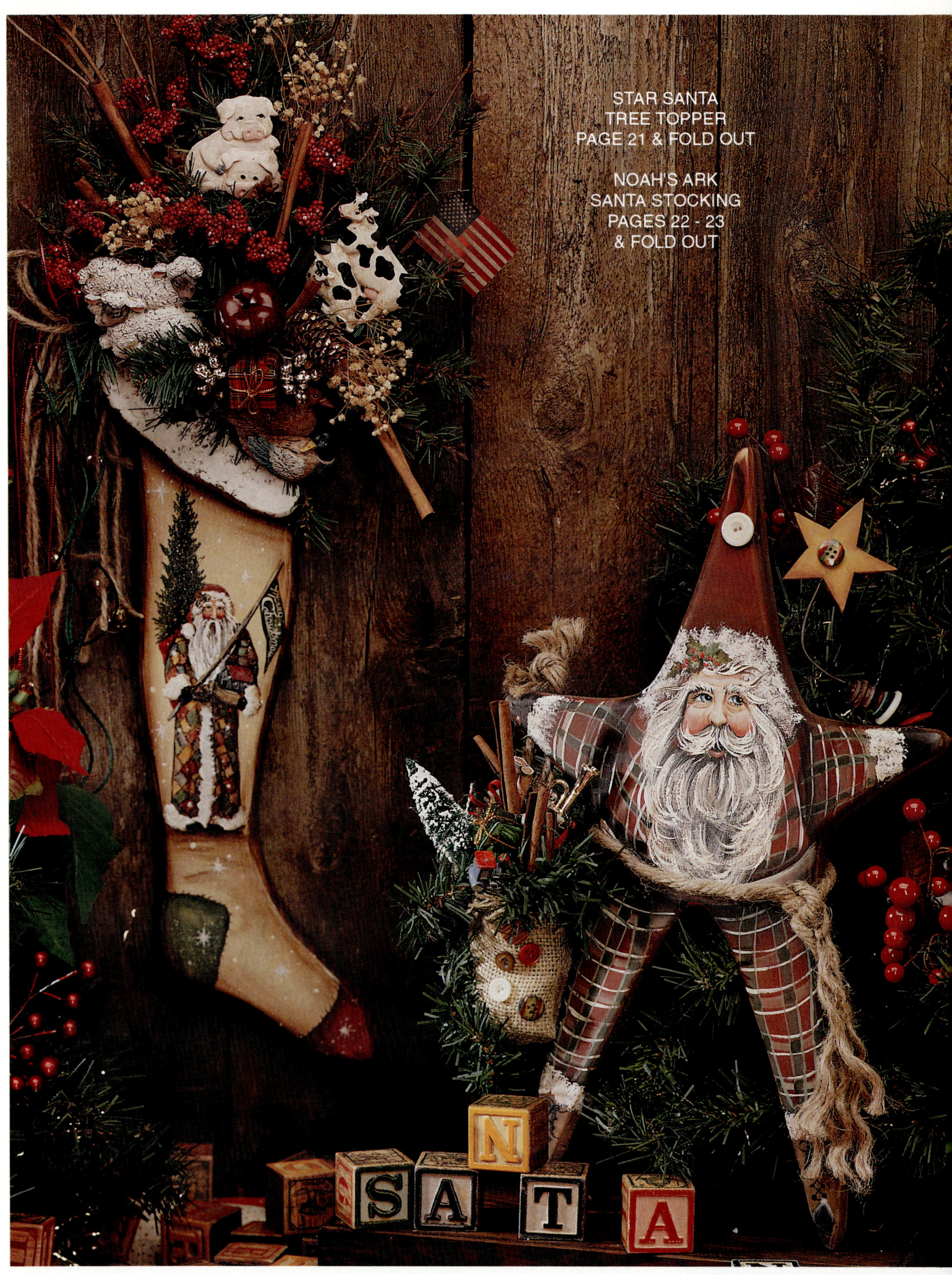

STAR SANTA
TREE TOPPER
PAGE 21 & FOLD OUT

NOAH'S ARK
SANTA STOCKING
PAGES 22 - 23
& FOLD OUT

Cookies for Santa
Snow Scene Plate

*These plates are painted with Apple Barrel Acrylic Gloss Enamel directly
on an inexpensive white plate.
Very durable and a great gift and family heirloom.*

PALETTE

Goodnight Blue   Real Green

Crown Gold   Coffee Bean

Black   White

Real Red

BRUSHES

No. 4 Flat Shader

1/4 Inch Angler

No. 00 Liner

1/2 Inch Flat Glaze Brush

INSTRUCTIONS

1. **PREPARATION:** Wash plate in hot soapy water. Rinse and dry well. Transfer pattern as needed.

2. **HILLS:** Using 1/2 inch glaze brush sideload in White and float hills in walking your color down as you paint.

3. **TREES:** Using angler and a touch of Real Green and Goodnight Blue - pounce - blend on palette and pounce tree in. Pick up more White of Goodnight Blue as needed (refer to photo).

4. **HOUSE:** Basecoat house (one coat give a nice look) with Crown Gold. Let dry. Shade with Coffee Bean, outline in Black. Roof is undercoated in Goodnight Blue. White is glazed over this. Doors Black, window grid is Black.

5. **TREE IN FRONT OF HOUSE:** Using double loaded angler with Goodnight Blue/Real Green pounce tree in. Reload angler tip with White and pounce snow on tips of limbs.

6. **PATH:** Undercoat (glaze) path in a touch of Goodnight Blue and Coffee Bean. Let dry. Re-glaze with sideloaded brush and White. Also Re-glaze all hills with White. Swirl White out of chimney.

7. **HOLLY:** Using No. 4 flat float holly in with Real Green, outline in Black. Berries are dotted in with handle of brush. Comma strokes and lettering are painted in using liner. Lettering is Real Red, outline to the right of all letters with Real Green. Spatter with White and a touch of Goodnight Blue giving a fresh fallen snow effect.

8. **LET DRY 24 HOURS.** Pre-heat oven to 350 degrees and bake in oven for 30 minutes. Turn oven off and let cool in oven. This helps set the paint and makes this piece very durable.

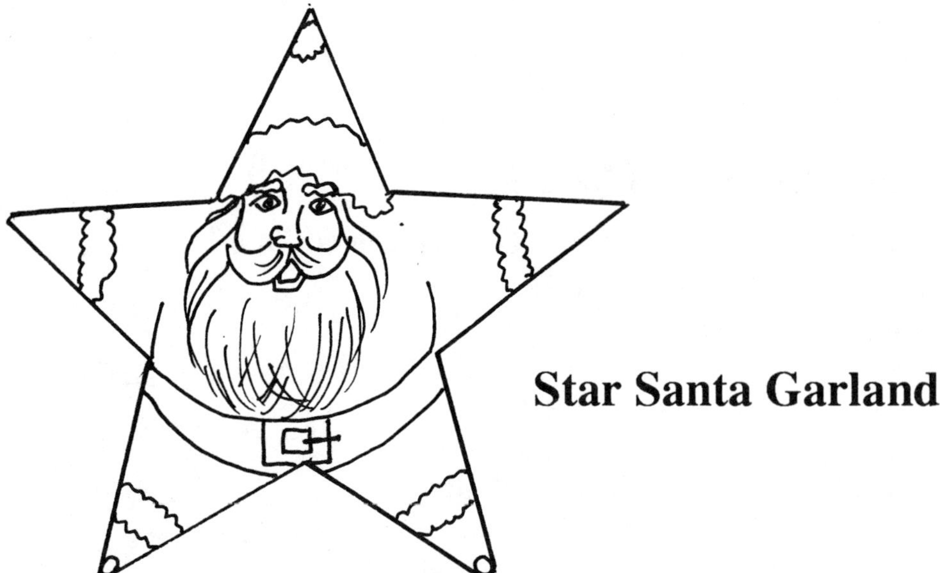

Star Santa Garland

Cookies for Santa Bear Wreath Plate

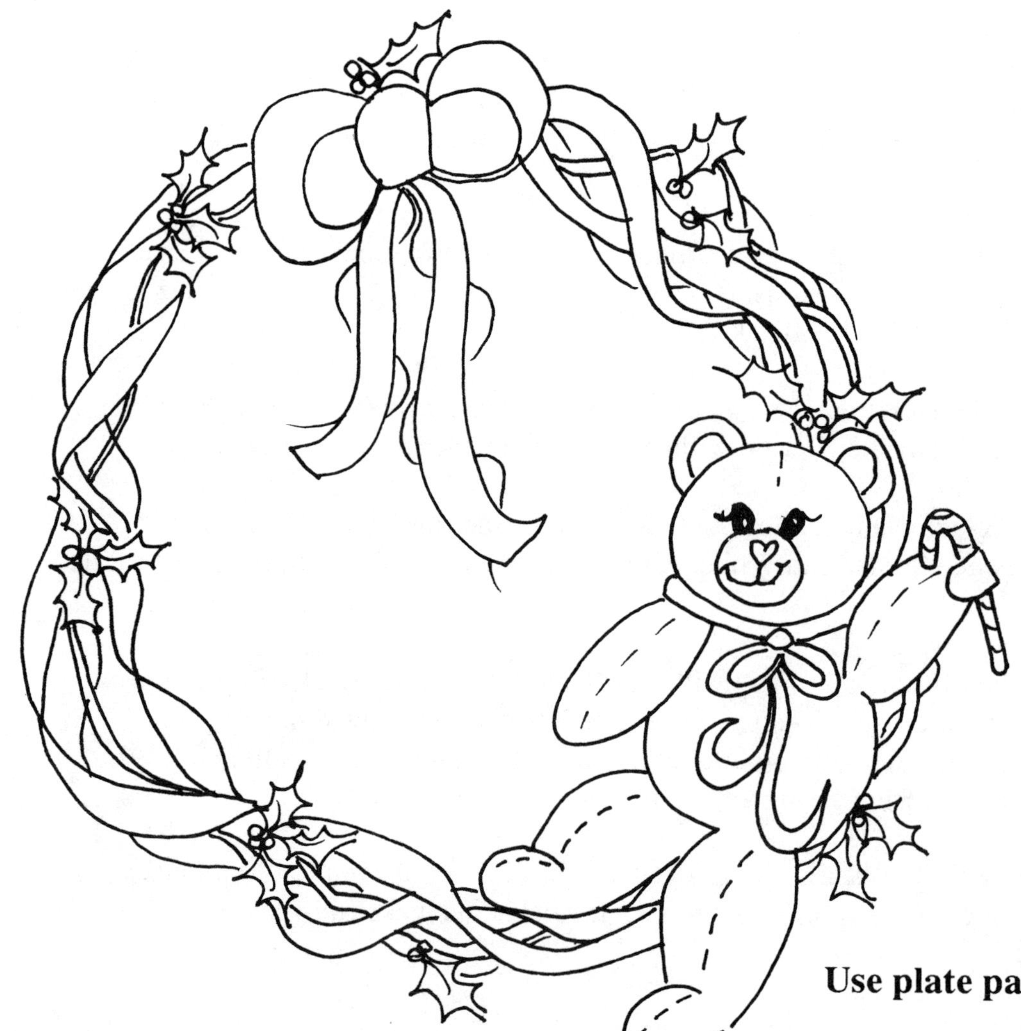

Use plate pattern for both projects

Cookies for Santa
Snow Scene Plate

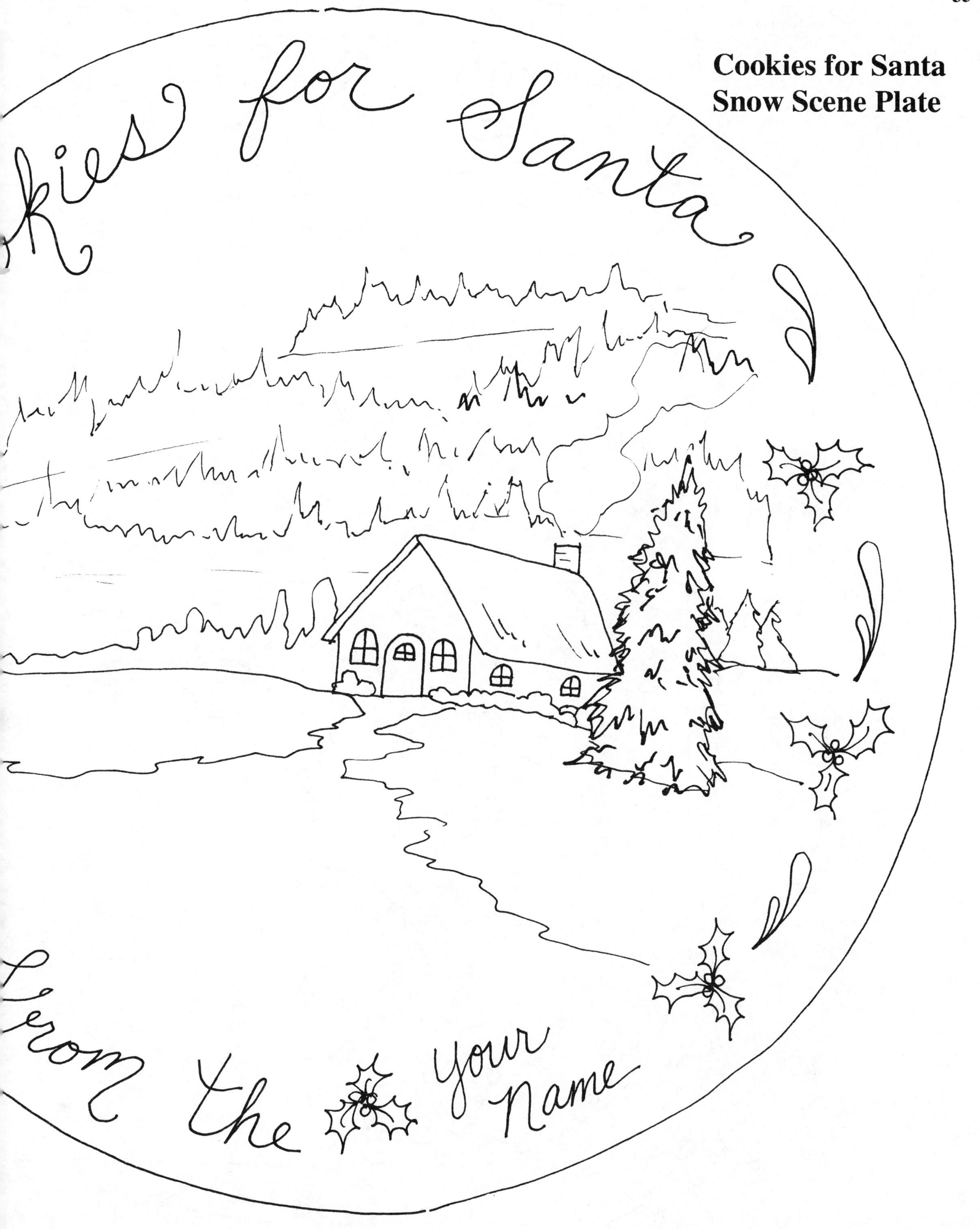

MERRY C
19

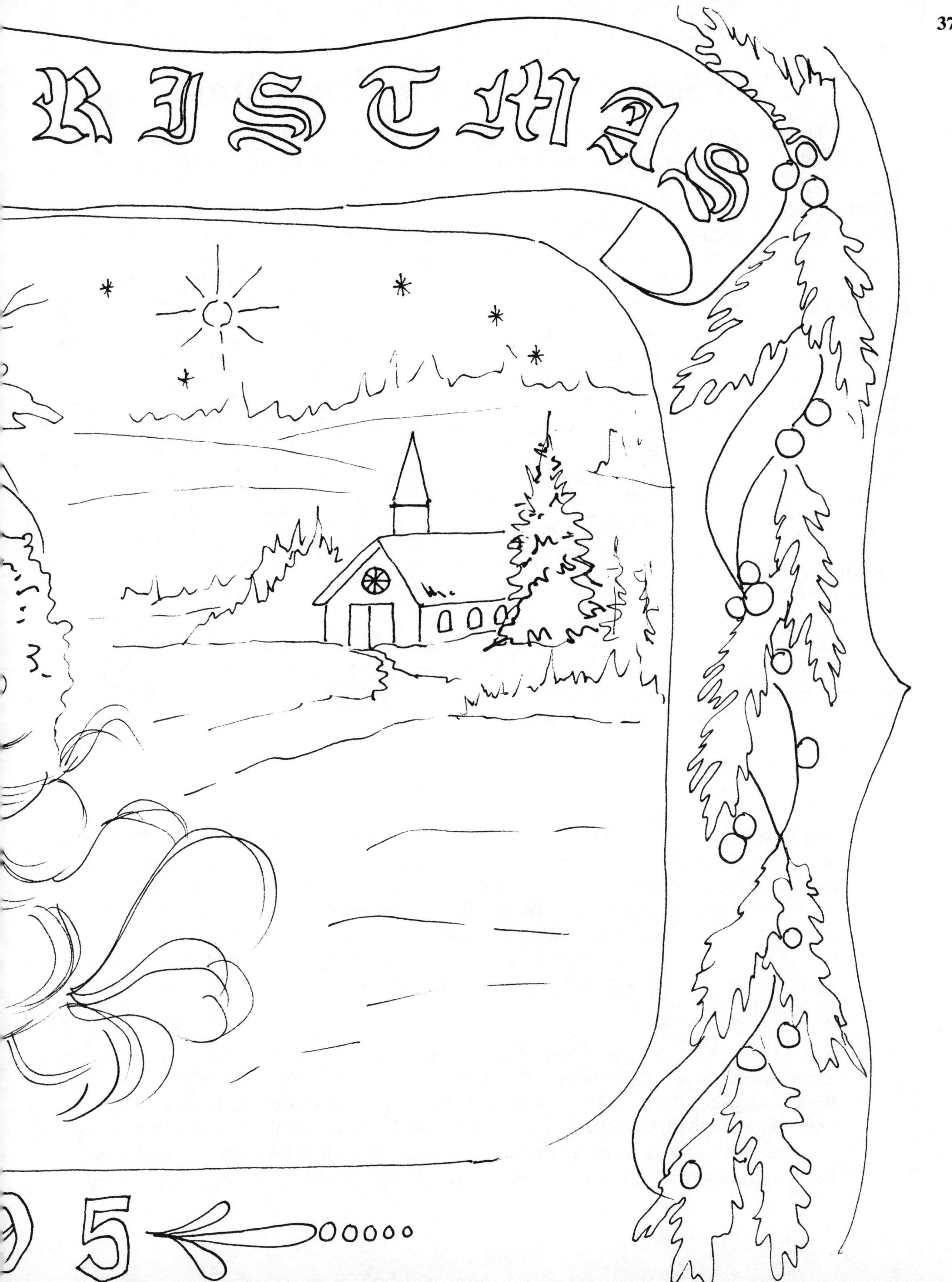
RISTMAS

1995 Saint Nicholas Christmas Tray

This tray could also be a beautiful Welcome Sign hanging on a door or fireplace. This is my second collectible "plate", hope you enjoy painting it!!

MATERIALS
#556 12 x 16 Chippendale Tray - Available through Walnut Hollow Farm; many craft shops carry this versatile piece also.

PALETTE
Burnt Carmine	Metallic Gold
Southern Pine	Christmas Red
Cherry Royale	Red Light
Yellow Ochre	Molasses
Emerald Isle	Almond Parfait
Burnt Umber	Portrait Dark
Midnight	Thunder Blue
Licorice	Taffy
Red Violet	Wicker White

BRUSHES
3/4 Inch Glaze	No. 10 Flat Shader
Script Liner	No. 2 Flat Shader
1/2 Inch Filbert Rake	1 Inch Stencil Brush (To basecoat center of plate)
No. 4 Flat Shader	2 Inch Sponge Brush (To basecoat outer edge of plate)

5/8 Inch Angle Shader (Trees and greenery)
Small stencil brush or old scruffy brush to pounce fur in with.

MISCELLANEOUS
Waterbase Varnish

1. **PREPARATION:** Sand and tack wood piece. Use a 1 inch stencil brush double loaded with Midnight and Thunder Blue. Paint this color 1/3 way down inside of tray - wipe this out of the brush - pick up Red Violet and work this in the center areas (working from left to right). wipe this color out of brush; pick up more Thunder Blue plus touch of Taffy, work this to the bottom. Let dry. Paint outer edge of tray with a double loaded 2 inch sponge brush (Red Light on outside edge -Burnt Carmine on inside edge, blending gently together). Pressure your sponge brush on plate edge and "rub" paint in smooth sweeps. Let dry. Sand with paper sack. Transfer pattern.

2. **BACKGROUND:** Using your 3/4 inch glaze brush, float Taffy hills in. Using your angle brush load the tip with Taffy (pounce blend) tap trees in. Church is floated in with the No. 10 flat and Licorice. Windows are scant amount of Yellow Ochre, outlined with "inky" Taffy liner. Door is Red Light, outline Taffy. Roof is floated in Taffy - re-highlighted with Wicker White and touch of Yellow Ochre. Dry brush this same color where large star is painted in sky. Using liner, paint Wicker White stars in.

3. **SAINT NICHOLAS:** In painting order
    FACE: Basecoat face Almond Parfait - Let dry. Transfer facial features. Basecoat eyeball socket Wicker White. Shade face using Portrait Dark around perimeter of face; down right of nose; wrinkles on forehead; above eye socket; and bags under eyes. Re-shade randomly with Molasses.
    EYES: Float iris (left then right) in Midnight. Licorice pupil. Burnt Umber lashes. Wicker White sparkles in eyes.
    CHEEKS: Float with Christmas Red. Also float bottom tip of nose. Dry brush upper cheek bone with Taffy.
    COAT: Basecoat Cherry Royal, shade Burnt Carmine, highlight Red Light. Re-highlight with a touch of Taffy.
    FUR: Pounce with double loaded old scruffy brush, Burnt Umber/Taffy.
    BAG: Emerald Isle - shade Licorice, highlight Taffy.
    GLOVE: Burnt Umber, shade Licorice. Dry brush Yellow Ochre and touch of Taffy highlight.
    BEARD: Using filbert rake and a scant amount of Burnt Umber and a touch of Yellow Ochre, whisk them in. Now pick up a little Taffy (if this starts to drag, add water to stroke wisps in). Pick up more Taffy, then wisp this and finally Wicker White fine wisps.

4. **TREE IN ST. NICK'S BAG:** Do not clean brush out between colors. Using angle brush double loaded with Southern Pine/Yellow Ochre (dark on short end-light on long end) pounce some of this in, then pick up a little Taffy and highlight some. Burnt Umber and Emerald Isle - pounce some of this in and highlight with touch of Taffy as needed. Using No. 2 flat double loaded with Yellow Ochre and Burnt Umber, paint in pine cones. Christmas Red berries dotted in with handle end of brush. Liner brush inky Taffy limbs complete the tree.

5. **WELCOME SCROLL:** "Streak" basecoat with Taffy and Yellow Ochre. Shade with Molas ses. Shade underside with Burnt Umber. Shade under scroll with Burnt Carmine. Stencil or paint wording in Emerald Isle.

6. **GOLD RIBBON:** Using a No. 10 shader, dip in water and blot on paper towel, dip into Metallic Gold and paint ribbon in.

7. **PINE BOUGHS:** Use the angle brush and pounce boughs in same colors as St. Nick's tree.

8. **RED BERRIES:** Use the No. 4 flat shader double loaded with Red Light and Burnt Carmine, highlight some with Taffy, others with touch of Yellow Ochre.

9. Using liner intertwine Metallic Gold though the boughs.

10. **FINISH:** Spatter inside plate with Wicker White (snow flakes). Let dry. Varnish all with waterbase varnish.

Now stand back and admire your work. You can almost hear the wind and snow blowing St. Nick's beard and tree as he trudges through the night for those important deliveries.

Susan Scheewe Publications, Inc.

ACRYLIC BOOKS

Vol. 19	"Gift of Painting" by Susan Scheewe	230	$8.50___
Vol. 1	"Painting It's Our Bag" by Bev Hink/Susan Scheewe	193	$8.50___
Vol. 4	"Keepsake Sampler" by Susan & Camille Scheewe	200	$6.50___
Vol. 1	"Loving You" by Susan & Camille Scheewe	244	$7.50___
Vol. 1	"Keepsakes For The Holidays" by Charleen Stempel & Susan Scheewe	286	$8.50___
Vol. 1	"Mrs. MacGregor's Garden" by Charleen Stempel & Susan Scheewe	316	$8.50___
Vol. 1	"Kids And Water" by Joyce Benner	234	$8.50___
Vol. 2	"The Flower Market" by Joyce Benner	319	$8.50___
Vol. 1	"Natures Palette" by Carol Binford	248	$8.50___
Vol. 1	"Country Fixin's" by Rhonda Caldwell	307	$8.50___
Vol. 2	"Country Fixin's - Sunflower Friends" by Rhonda Caldwell	321	$8.50___
Vol. 3	"Country Fixin's - For All Seasons" by Rhonda Caldwell	332	$8.50___
Vol. 1	"Santas and Sams" by Bobi Dolara	258	$8.50___
Vol. 2	"Vintage Peace" by Bobi Dolara	270	$8.50___
Vol. 1	"Floral Designs" by Carol Empet	312	$8.50___
Vol. 1	"Romantically Tole Bauernmalerei" by Sherry Gall	311	$8.50___
Vol. 1	"Holiday Gathering" by Angie Hupp	267	$8.50___
Vol. 2	"Holiday Gathering" by Angie Hupp	292	$8.50___
Vol. 3	"Heavenly Gathering" by Angie Hupp	320	$8.50___
Vol. 1	"Happy Heart, Happy Home" by Cathy Jones	241	$7.50___
Vol. 1	"Pickets & Pastimes" by Marie & Jim King	329	$8.50___
Vol. 3	"Country's Edge" by Shirley Koenig...O/AC	291	$8.50___
Vol. 1	"Huckleberry Horse" by Hanna Long	269	$8.50___
Vol. 1	"Love Lives Here" by Mary Lynn Lewis	170	$6.50___
Vol. 2	"Love Lives Here" by Mary Lynn Lewis	185	$6.50___
Vol. 3	"Love Lives Here" by Mary Lynn Lewis	195	$6.50___
Vol. 1	"Special Welcomes" by Corinne Miller	287	$8.50___
Vol. 2	"Special Welcomes" by Corinne Miller	298	$8.50___
Vol. 3	"Special Welcomes #3, Crazy About Crafting" by Corinne Miller	309	$8.50___
Vol. 4	"Special Welcomes #4 Farm-N-Friends" by Corinne Miller	324	$8.50___
Vol. 5	"Special Welcomes #5 All Wrapped Up" by Corinne Miller	333	$8.50___
Vol. 1	"Change With The Seasons, Wire Loops" by Joanna Miller	331	$8.50___
Vol. 1	"Fruit & Flower Fantasies" by Joyce Morrison	277	$8.50___
Vol. 1	"Wildflower Sampler" by Bev Norman	191	$8.50___
Vol. 1	"Whimsical Critters" by Lori Ohlson	228	$7.50___
Vol. 2	"Sunflower Farm" by Lori Ohlson	326	$8.50___
Vol. 1	"Holiday Medley" by Nina Owens	265	$8.50___
Vol. 2	"Another Holiday Medley" by Nina Owens	296	$8.50___
Vol. 1	"Oh Those Little Rascals" by Diane Permenter	247	$7.50___
Vol. 6	"Acrylic Charms" by Sharon Rachal	305	$8.50___
Vol. 1	"Forever In My Heart" by Diane Richards.....AC/Fabric	188	$6.50___
Vol. 2	"Memories In My Heart" by Diane Richards.....AC/Fabric	189	$6.50___
Vol. 3	"Forever In My Heart II" by Diane Richards.....AC/Fabric	205	$7.50___
Vol. 6	"Angels In My Stocking" by Diane Richards	254	$7.50___
Vol. 7	"Nostalgic Dreams" by Diane Richards	273	$8.50___
Vol. 1	"Second Time Around" by Sally Sauermilch	297	$8.50___
Vol. 2	"Second Time Around" by Sally Sauermilch	318	$8.50___
Vol. 1	"Holiday Hangarounds" by Marsha Sellers	327	$8.50___
Vol. 1	"Creations In Canvas...and More" by Carol Spooner	256	$7.50___
Vol. 1	"Gran's Garden" by Ros Stallcup	295	$8.50___
Vol. 2	"Another Gran's Garden" by Ros Stallcup	315	$8.50___
Vol. 3	"Gran's Garden & House" by Ros Stallcup	334	$8.50___
Vol. 1	"Christmas Greetings from the Cottage" by Chris Stokes	336	$8.50___
Vol. 1	"Christmas Visions" by Max Terry	278	$8.50___
Vol. 2	"Christmas Presence" by Max Terry	285	$8.50___
Vol. 3	"Painting Clay Pot-pourri" by Max Terry	310	$8.50___
Vol. 1	"Country Primitives" by Maxine Thomas	274	$8.50___
Vol. 2	"Country Primitives 2" by Maxine Thomas	300	$8.50___
Vol. 3	"Country Primitives 3" by Maxine Thomas	322	$8.50___
Vol. 1	"Rise & Shine" by Jolene Thompson	214	$6.50___
Vol. 2	"Garden Gate" by Jolene Thompson	250	$7.50___
Vol. 3	"Count Your Blessings" by Chris Thornton	196	$6.50___
Vol. 5	"Count Your Blessings" by Chris Thornton	213	$8.50___
Vol. 6	"Share Your Blessings" by Chris Thornton	226	$8.50___
Vol. 7	"Blessings" by Chris Thornton	255	$8.50___
Vol. 8	"Christmas Blessings" by Chris Thornton	266	$8.50___
Vol. 9	"Blessings For The Home" by Chris Thornton	275	$8.50___
Vol. 10	"Bazaar Blessings" by Chris Thornton	299	$8.50___
Vol. 11	"Painted Blessings" by Chris Thornton	323	$8.50___
Vol. 1	"Barnyard Friends" by Lou Ann Trice	306	$8.50___
Vol. 5	"Daydreams & Sweet Shirts II" by Don & Lynn Weed	208	$7.50___
Vol. 1	"Connie's Favorite Old-Time Labels" by Connie Williams	335	$8.50___
Vol. 1	"Floral Fabrics and Watercolor" by Sally Williams	262	$8.50___
Vol. 1	"A Time For Giving" by Evelyn Wright	308	$8.50___

****

SHIPPING & HANDLING CHARGES
Add $2.50 for the First Book for shipping and handling.

Add $1.50 per each additional book.

Please Add $3.00 for handling & postage. PER TAPES. Sorry we must have a "NO RE-FUND - NO RETURN" policy.

U.S CURRENCY

PRICES SUBJECT TO CHANGE WITHOUT NOTICE.

WE ACCEPT VISA & MASTERCARD

FOR MORE INFORMATION ON BOOKS OR SUPPLIES CALL OR WRITE US

WE ARE ALWAYS GLAD TO HEAR FROM YOU!

9-26-95

13435 N.E. Whitaker Way Portland, Or. 97230 PH (503) 254-9100 FAX (503) 252-9508

MORE FABULOUS BOOKS FROM SCHEEWE PUBLICATIONS

Books Retail For $8.50 each

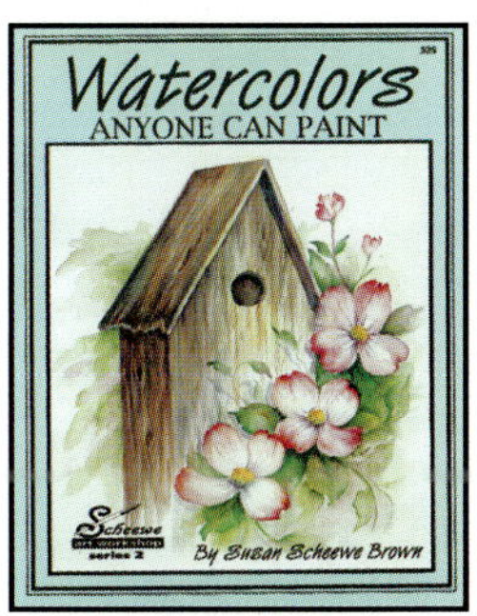

Watercolors
Anyone Can Paint
Susan Scheewe Brown
#325   Retail $11.95

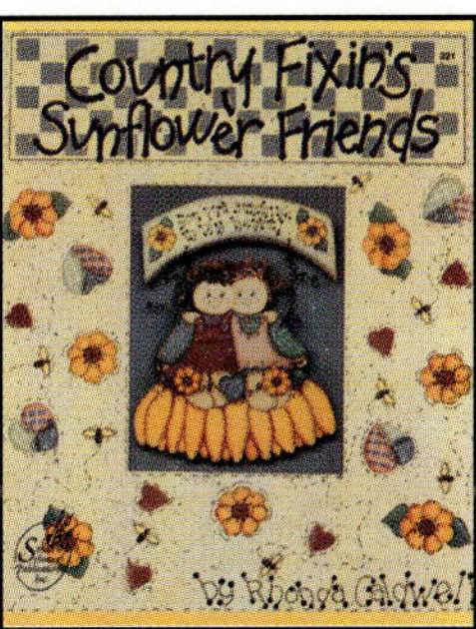

Country Fixin's 2
Sunflower Friends
Rhonda Caldwell #321
Acrylic

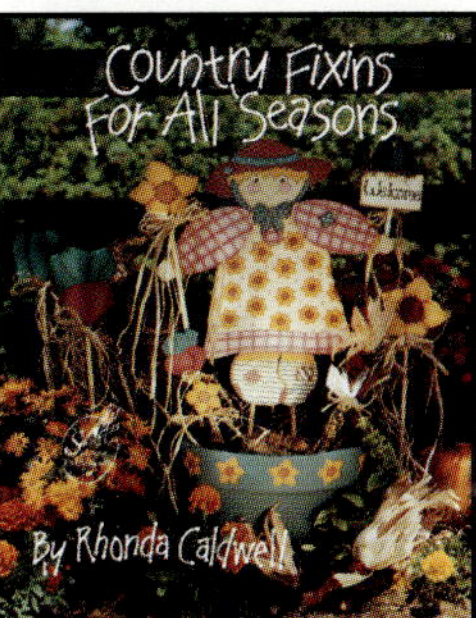

Country Fixin's 3
For All Seasons
Rhonda Caldwell #332
Acrylic

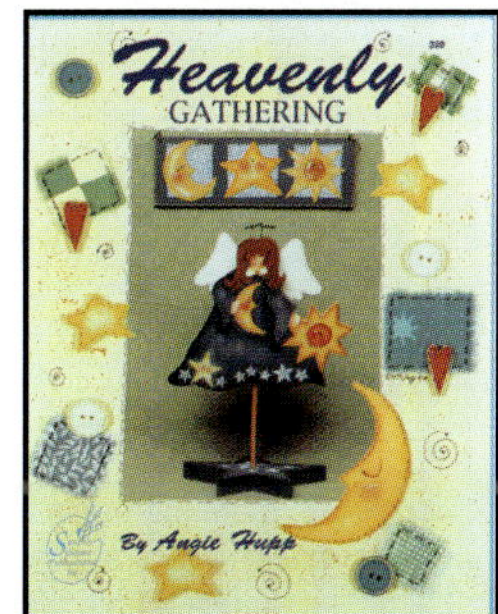

Heavenly Gathering
Angie Hupp # 320
Acrylic

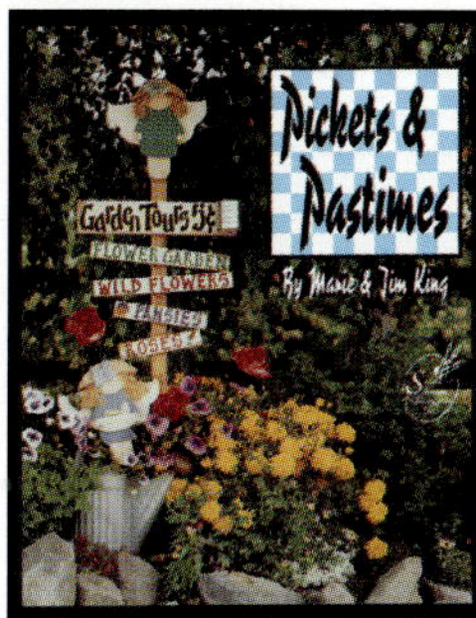

Pickets & Pastimes
Marie & Jim King #329
Acrylic

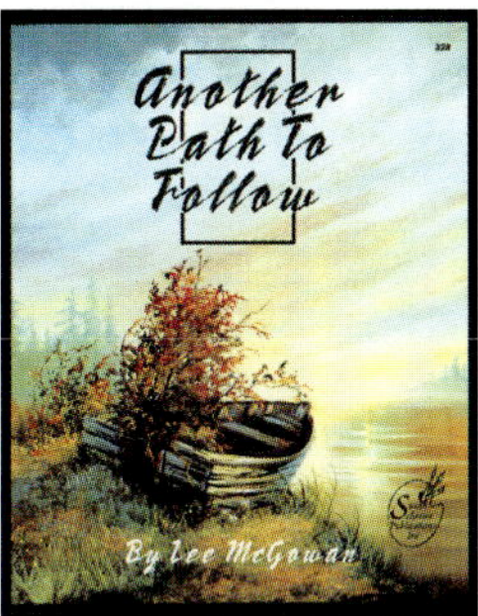

Another Path To Follow
Lee McGowen #328
Oil

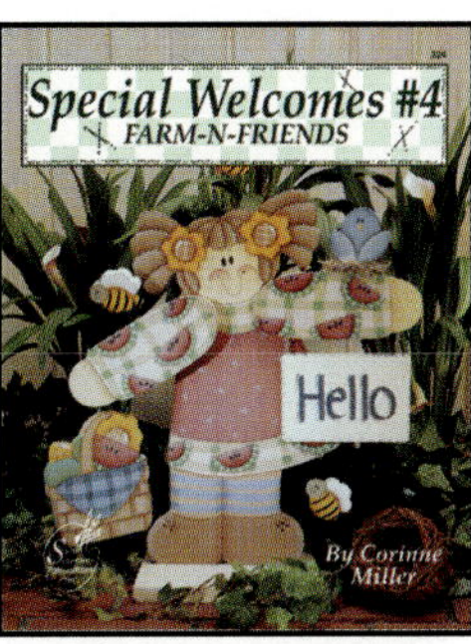

Special Welcomes 4
Farm-n-Friends
Corinne Miller #324
Acrylic

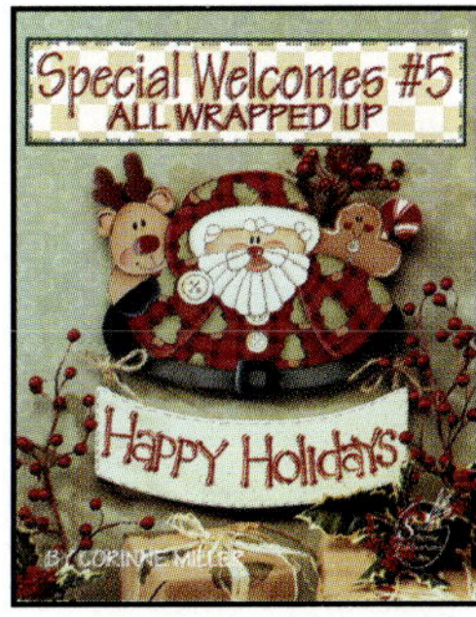

Special Welcomes 5
All Wrapped Up
Corinne Miller #333
Acrylic

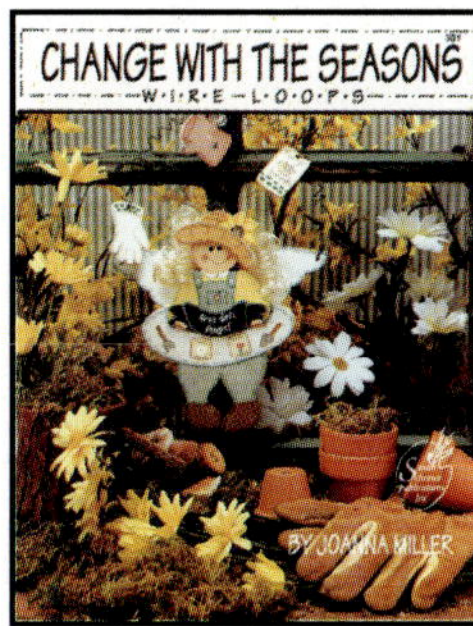

Change With The
Seasons Wire Loops
Joanne Miller #331
Acrylic

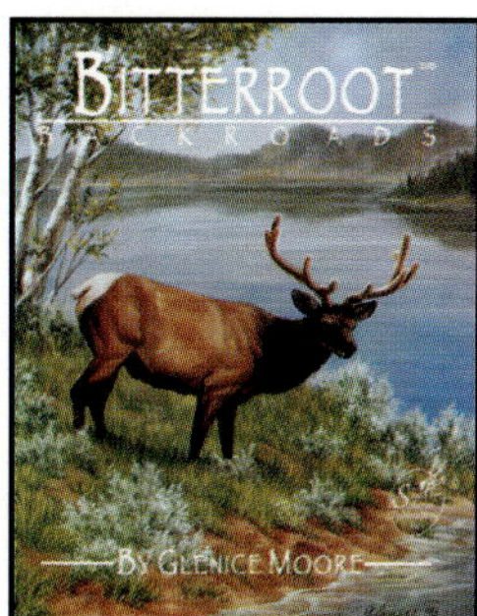

Bitterroot Backroads
Glenice Moore #330
Oil

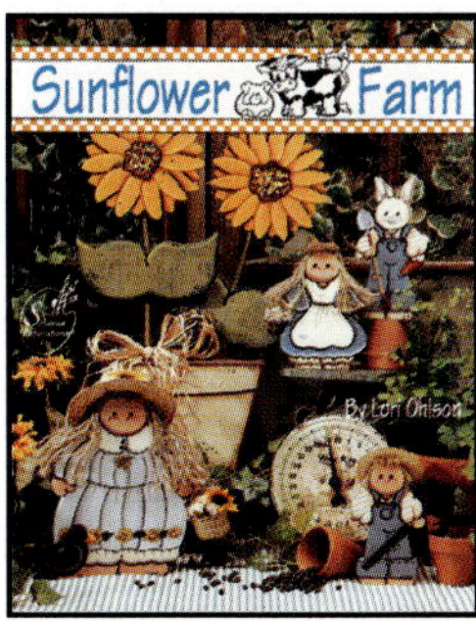

Sunflower Farm
Lori Ohlson #326
Acrylic

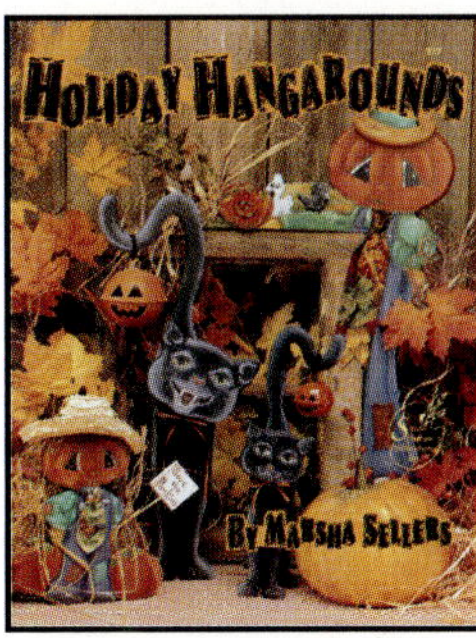

Holiday Hangarounds
Marsha Sellers #327
Acrylic

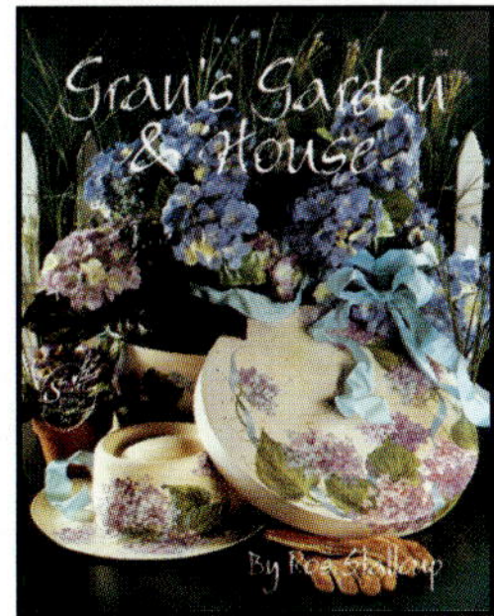

Gran's House & Garden
Ros Stallcup #334
Acrylic

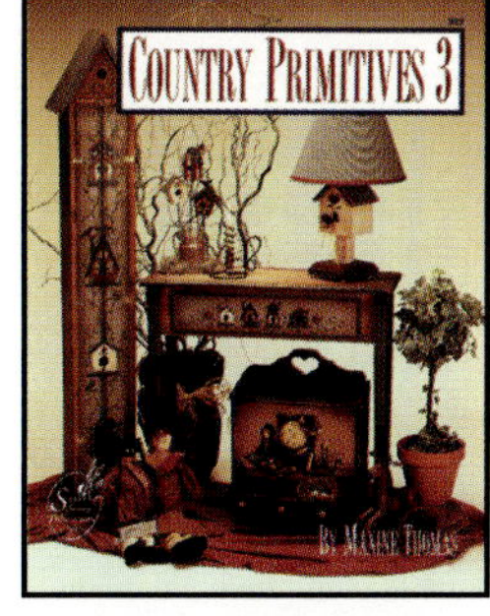

Country Primitives 3
Maxine Thomas #322
Acrylic

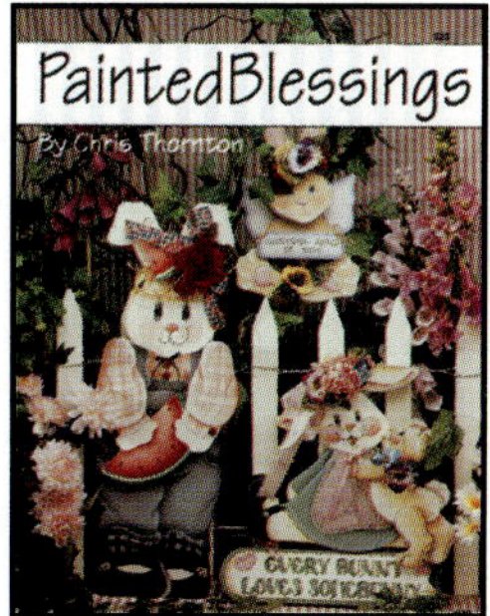

Painted Blessings
Chris Thornton #323
Acrylic

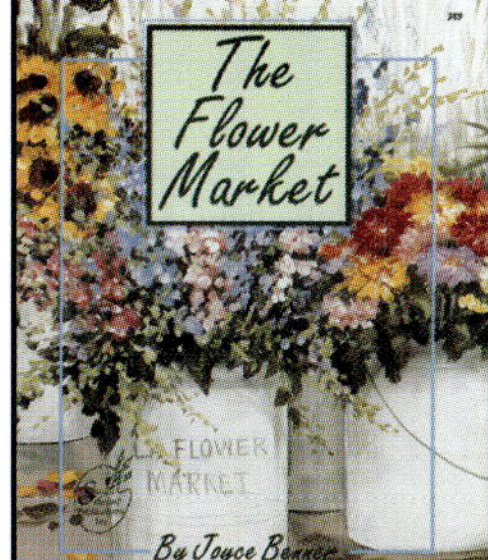

Flower Market
Joyce Benner #319
Acrylic

Ask for these and other Scheewe Publications at your local craft store.

Send $2.50 for the
First book for shipping
and handling.

Add $1.50 per additional
book shipping,
U.S. CURRENCY

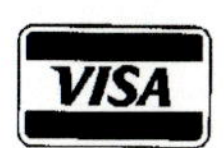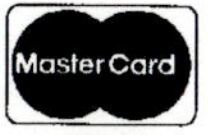

WELCOMED

Order Direct By Phone or Mail

Scheewe Publications Inc.

13435 N.E. Whitaker Way
Portland, Or. 97230
PH (503) 254-9100 FAX (503) 252-9508

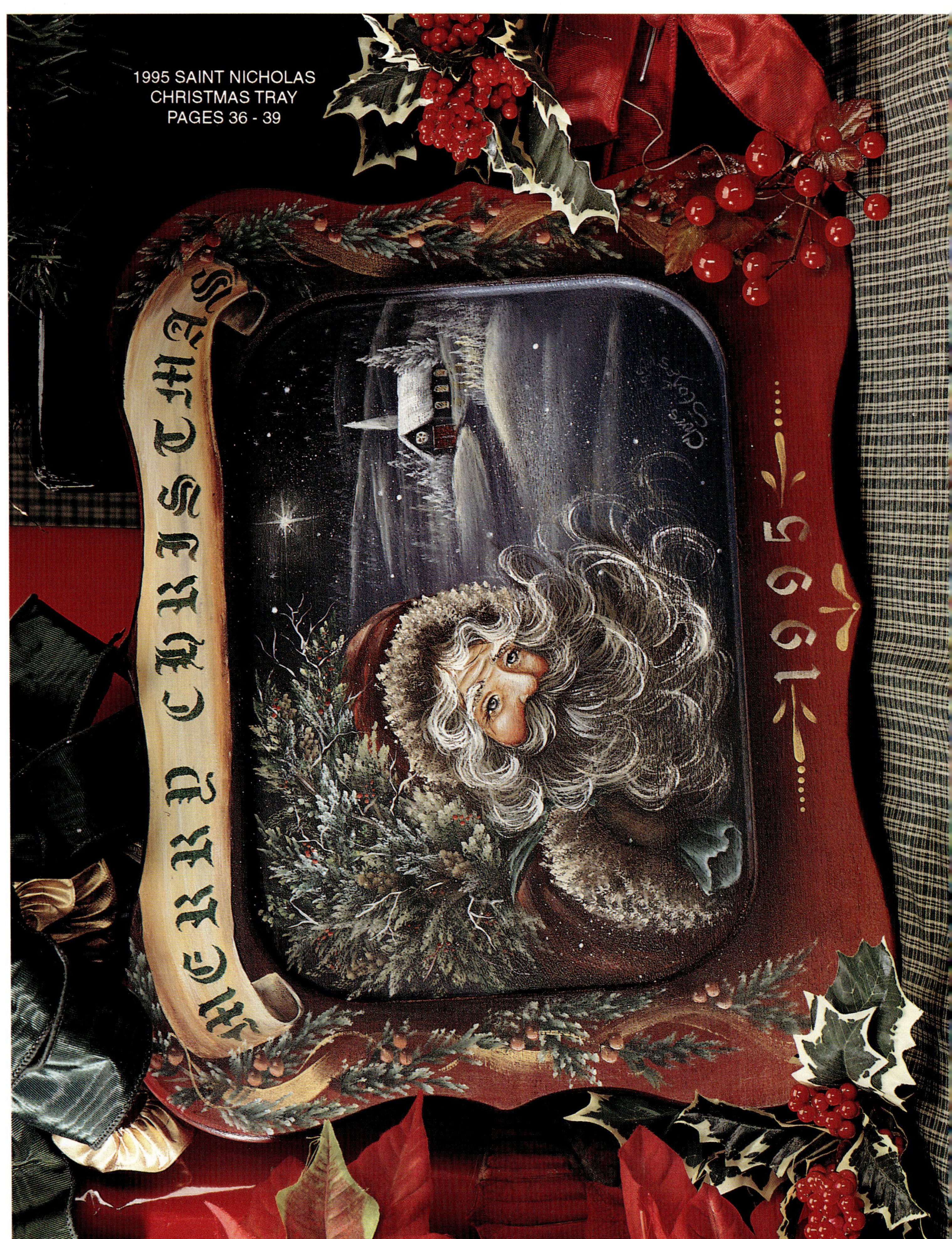

1995 SAINT NICHOLAS
CHRISTMAS TRAY
PAGES 36 - 39
MERRY CHRISTMAS
1995